Contents

Foreword

Memories That Matter is a book about discovering oneself. Jefferson Singer wonders, in his opening sentence, "If I asked you who you are, what would you say?" Perhaps not surprisingly—or *Memories That Matter* would be the briefest of volumes—this turns out to be a deceptively simple question that in fact is psychologically complicated and quite fascinating. Jefferson describes how our identities—indeed, our understanding of ourselves and our social worlds—are organized by a set of especially vivid stories that we repetitively tell about ourselves; these *self-defining memories* synthesize our goals, thoughts, and feelings, giving life to a coherent and recognizable personality. A gifted researcher, educator, and psychotherapist, Jefferson analyzes the personal memories of participants in his research program, his clients from his private practice, and even his own grandmother to reveal insights about the role of these memories in determining the characteristic ways in which we relate to other people, achieve (or fail to achieve) intimacy, understand ourselves, deal with triumphs and losses, and lead a creative life.

The title of this book, *Memories That Matter*, reminds us that it is not just any memory that is significant, but that certain recollections are especially influential. There is a set of self-defining memories that psychologically link together our motives, belief systems, and characteristic ways of responding emotionally to events in our lives. So this is a book that concerns, in a way, the relationship of passion and reason,

vi   Memories That Matter

a puzzle that has intrigued philosophers for centuries and fueled my own laboratory's work on what we have called *emotional intelligence*.[1]

In Jefferson's and my first year of graduate school, we met and discovered the writings of the late psychologist Sylvan Tomkins. One of his passages in particular left a memorable impression. "Out of the marriage of reason with affect there issues clarity with passion," Tomkins wrote. "Reason without affect would be impotent, affect without reason would be blind."[2] In his ideas about scripts, which Jefferson summarizes later in this book, Tomkins began to describe a way in which affect and reason could be tied together in shaping our personalities. *Memories That Matter*, drawing on the important developments in the field of psychology since Tomkins, leads you on a journey that will help you to understand how passion and reason are connected in your own sense of yourself.

Obviously the ideas in this book resonate with my own research interests; I find them fascinating and stimulating scientifically, and they have led as well to new insights about my personal sense of my own identity. However, I am delighted to add these prefatory words to *Memories That Matter* for another reason. Jefferson Singer and I occupied an office together in Yale University's Kirtland Hall from our first day in graduate school until we completed our doctoral dissertations some years later. And that propinquity led to a deep friendship. Within, Jefferson describes for you a little about those early days of learning to think like psychologists. We shared an interest in the psychology of emotions, rockabilly music, and baseball (although Jefferson is a Yankee fan while I root for the Red Sox).

Perhaps not surprisingly, Jefferson is the source of many of my personal memories, and some that are self-defining. I have clear recollections of sitting on his porch listening to baseball games on the radio, an image that reminds me of the desirability of simple pleasures even in a hectic and multimedia world and motivates me to seek them in my current life. Conversations about old-time country music led to my accessing a dream of playing bass in a bluegrass band—despite never having played a note—and these were the source of a later desire to learn how to play the instrument and organize the Professors of Bluegrass, Yale's student-faculty bluegrass band. A memory of listening to music on his parents' stereo and playing along on his brother's one-string, washtub bass is a self-defining one for me; recruiting that memory brings about pleasurable emotions that then motivate my enjoyment of creating music with others and learning to play my instrument better. And, of course, sharing ideas with Jeff about psychology as graduate students twenty-five years ago and now as middle-aged professors continues to stimulate new connections and approaches in my own work.

My final point, quite simply, is this: Jefferson Singer has been an important thinker and influential friend in shaping how I see myself and my worldview. Our relationship has, in part, helped me to figure out who I am. Even if you never have the privilege to get to know Jefferson personally, reading *Memories That Matter* will bring you into closer contact with him in ways that I suspect will be life-transforming for you too. Enjoy his wonderful stories and his uniquely synthetic ideas about human psychology. Try some of the exercises he outlines here. You will not think about yourself in the same ways again. Since meeting Jefferson, I know I haven't!

—Peter Salovey
Dean of Yale College
Chris Argyris Professor of Psychology Yale University
New Haven, Connecticut September 2005

[1] Salovey, P., & Mayer, J.D. 1990. Emotional intelligence. *Imagination, Cognition, and Personality*, 9, 185-211.

[2] Tomkins, S.S. 1962. *Affect, imagery, and consciousness, Volume 1, The positive affects.* New York: Springer, p. 112.

Acknowledgments

I agreed to start this project while in the midst of writing another book about the role of personality psychology in psychotherapy. If I had not worked with such a helpful and efficient staff at New Harbinger, I would never had been able to complete this book and find it such an engaging and pleasurable experience. I would like first to thank Matt McKay for asking me to develop a book on self-defining memories for a more general readership. He has been a supportive influence as this book has taken shape. I would like to acknowledge the editorial expertise of Melissa Kirk, who guided me to fit my ideas and writing into the New Harbinger style. Our correspondences and conversations about title possibilities, chapter structure, and focus were critical to my work. I appreciate the thoughtful manuscript editing and feedback from Heather Mitchener, as well as the careful copyediting of Claire Splan. Thanks are also due to Amy Shoup for her attractive and creative cover.

I would like to acknowledge the ongoing support of my colleagues in the psychology department of Connecticut College and our department administrator, Nancy MacLeod, who, as with all my other books, has provided invaluable support and assistance. I would like to recognize the many contributions of my graduate student and research assistant, Jenna Baddeley, who helped with all phases of this book, including providing thoughtful editorial feedback on chapter drafts.

I would like to acknowledge the debt I owe to fellow researchers in the fields of personality and memory whose work has markedly influenced this book—Dan McAdams, Robert Emmons, Martin Conway, Susan Bluck, and Avril Thorne. I would like to thank my longtime friend and collaborator Peter Salovey for his kindness in writing a foreword to this book.

Finally, I would like to thank my parents, both for their general influence on my work in psychology and more specifically for their early discussions with me about the direction this book might take. As always, I am deeply grateful to my wife, Anne, and my daughters, Olivia and Chloe, for their patience with me whenever I would ask for just a little more time to finish a chapter. Anne has been a helpful reader and source of advice for many of the sections of this book. The reader will also see that some of my daughters' memories are featured in this work. No debt can repay Anne and them, nor my parents, brothers, and friends, for providing me with the memories that matter most in my own life.

Introduction

If I asked you who you are, what would you say? You might say your name or what you look like or what you do for a living. You might say your religious affiliation, your most important beliefs, and your favorite activities. These are important parts of you, but if I really wanted to know who you are, you would probably want to tell me something about your past. You would probably want to share stories of the big events, good or bad, that have happened in your life. You might talk about an important relationship or about one of your proudest achievements. You might describe a conflict with a family member or an illness that you overcame.

All of these stories are based on memories—memories that convey what has mattered most to you in your life. By sharing these important memories with me, you are letting me know about the experiences that have made you who you are today. These memories have a power and meaning that psychologists have only recently begun to understand and study systematically. The goal of this book is to share these recent scientific insights about memory with you and then show how you can put them to work in your current life.

One of the biggest experiences in my twelve-year-old daughter Chloe's life was our recent move from the small town in which she was born. The first few months were very difficult for her, filled with confusion, tears, and homesickness. One night she had a sleepover at our new home with two of her old friends from our former town and one girl from our new community. The two old friends, who had known Chloe all their lives, were trying to describe her to the new friend. Suddenly, one of them began to imitate Chloe's nightly ritual for going to bed, and before she got through two words the other friend chimed in with the exact same words and cadence. "Goodnight Mom, goodnight Dad, goodnight Olivia [her sister], goodnight everyone. I love you all so much. See you in the morning. Goodnight, goodnight, goodnight— Goodniiiight!!!!"

Their imitation was so perfect that we were literally crying with laughter. Yet despite the teasing, they were conveying to the new friend an essential point about who Chloe was. Beneath her stylish jeans and hoop earrings, Chloe has remained a sweet and innocent kid who likes everyone to be safe and all things to be in their right place. Her friends' memory of how she ends each day said much more about who Chloe is than any list of adjectives or description of her traits could ever do.

By learning to identify how simple memories like these express important truths, you can harness a greater understanding of yourself and the people that matter most to you. At the same time, you can learn how to make use of these memories for positive change in every aspect of your life.

All you will need to put these memories to work are the blank pages of a journal, a pen, and, most of all, the openness and honesty to look inside and draw on the full range of your past experiences. The power of your personal memories lies in your willingness to recall and explore both joyous and sorrowful events. The more open you are to reviewing the various memories of your life, the more you are likely to learn and the more opportunity you will have to change and grow. In this way your past can be a prologue to a better future.

WHAT YOU WILL GAIN FROM THIS BOOK

This book provides you with the fruits of over twenty years of research and clinical work focused on the role of personal memories in individuals' lives. Researchers and psychotherapists have uncovered vital links between memories and:

- Repetitive relationship patterns

- Life goals

- Personal meaning

- Loss

- Creativity

- Intimacy

In the chapters that follow, you will learn in straightforward language about these connections, as illustrated by case studies and descriptions of research findings. More importantly, each chapter shows you how to benefit in your own life from this information. Each chapter is filled with practical exercises that take you step-by-step through the process of identifying your important personal memories and then learning how to put them to use for self-understanding, positive action, and personal growth.

By working your way through the chapters of this book, you will gain:

- Greater ability to recall memories in a vivid and emotional manner

- Better understanding of how memories affect relationships

- The skill to draw on memories for life success

- Greater self-knowledge and wisdom from your memories

- Control over memories of loss and grief

- Mastery of memories for problem solving and creativity

- Techniques for using memory to enhance intimacy and excitement

If this list sounds ambitious, be assured that the examples and recommendations offered in the chapters ahead are based on actual research and clinical work. You will meet several individuals in this volume no different from yourself who have applied techniques described in these pages and achieved positive results in their lives. By working diligently to employ the various memory techniques, they have gained better control over their memories. They have learned how to minimize the self-defeating and undermining aspects of memory and maximize the aspects that encourage and promote growth.

Since our daily thoughts cannot avoid drawing on personal memories, some of which may be extremely painful, we should recognize that if we don't take action to control memory's influence, we remain at risk for experiencing its more troubling and potentially debilitating effects. If we do not learn how to master our personal memories, they can:

- Block and interfere with our goals

- Obscure new insights and growth

- Take over and stifle our moods

- Rob us of our capacity for pleasure and intimacy

Given memory's potential for undermining your best hopes and efforts in life, you cannot afford to become its passive victim. By applying techniques from this volume, you can take control of your memory and direct it toward its most positive and healthy potential.

WHO SHOULD READ THIS BOOK

This is truly a book for anyone who wants make their personal memories a valuable asset in their life. In addition to the general reader, students with an interest in psychology or those pursuing training in counseling or psychotherapy may find it a useful source of ideas and techniques. The exercises in this book are based on actual therapeutic practice, so therapists might also find this book helpful to use as an adjunct to their work with particular clients.

For some readers new to the exploration of their personal memories, you may be wondering at this point if you are going to be able to locate important memories and to master the techniques that will allow you to learn from them. You need not worry—memories are the lifeblood of each and every person's mind. We could not be fully human without a capacity for memory, and though some of us may have more accurate or detailed memories than others, each of us has access to key memories that make us who we are and help to define what we want to become. With the few simple guidelines and exercises outlined in the following chapters, you will be ready to tap into this highly accessible resource for self-understanding and effective motivation. Beyond the price of this book (which you may have already paid), you will need no more expenditures, materials (other than your memory journal), or fancy training courses. There are no certificates to be earned, workshops to take, or requirements to satisfy. The only requisite is that you take the time to look inside yourself and begin to explore those most important memories. The result may be new strides in self-understanding and the harnessing of a powerful tool to help you change and grow.

THE CHAPTERS AHEAD

Chapter 1 takes you systematically through an understanding of the most important memories in your life—your self-defining memories. To make sense of what these memories are and how they work, I describe briefly how contemporary psychologists explain the workings of memory in general. With these fundamental principles in place, we then turn to self-defining memories. We review the five key elements of these memories and then work on an exercise to identify your own self-defining memories. Once you have located your memories, I ask you to consider carefully the different emotions that each memory awakens inside you.

In chapter 2 we consider how your self-defining memories are linked to the most important goals in your life. To make these connections, you will perform an exercise to uncover your most important personal goals. You then examine how your memories and goals overlap. You learn methods for maximizing the power of your memories to move you closer to your goals and to minimize any memory interference with what you are striving to accomplish.

Chapter 3 shows you how to uncover the most significant messages and meanings in your self-defining memories. You learn techniques for identifying the important themes and conflicts that are contained in your memories. You then learn techniques based in imagery and role-playing that will allow you to make these memory themes and conflicts sources of change and growth.

We take a look in chapter 4 at the role that self-defining memories play in your moods and emotions. You will learn how memory can either overcome or prolong negative moods in your life. You will learn straightforward strategies for putting your memories to work in maximizing positive moods and minimizing negative moods.

In chapter 5, we examine those memories that hurt the most and are hardest to move past. We look at what happens when memories of loss keep returning to your thoughts and cause you to feel stuck. We look at how to acknowledge loss and honor it, but also how to make sure that your memories of loss do not become an obstacle to growth and life's positive experiences. Although we acknowledge the significance of memories of lost loved ones, the goal of the exercises in this chapter is to help you regain greater control of your thoughts and feelings in order not to be overwhelmed by these memories.

In chapter 6, we explore the role of memory in pleasure, creativity, imagination, and as an aid in intimacy. Here you can see how writers and artists have relied on their personal memories as sources of inspiration. You will also learn techniques for using your self-defining memories to expand your own creative process and problem-solving abilities. Finally, you will learn how you and your partner can share memories and use imagery to enhance your sensual pleasure.

We finish in chapter 7 with a discussion of where your personal memories fit in across your whole life span. We trace the journey of memory from its beginnings at your birth to the legacy that you might leave to the generations that follow after you.

Across all of these chapters, we move from clear statements of scientific research and case studies to explanations of exercises and methods that you can apply in your own life. Each chapter can stand alone to help you focus on a particular aspect of memory, but the volume in its entirety provides you with a flexible tool chest to realize the greatest potential from your most important personal memories.

A FEW WORDS ABOUT THE SCIENCE BEHIND THIS BOOK

In the past twenty-five years there has been an explosion in the study of what psychologists call *autobiographical memory* or memories about events that you have experienced firsthand in your own life. Since autobiographical memory is a bit of a mouthful, psychologists often use the term *personal memory* to refer to the same kind of firsthand memories. With advances in neuroscience, cognitive science, and an interdisciplinary emphasis on narrative or storytelling across the disciplines of the social sciences and humanities, we are gaining remarkable insights into how personal memory works and the role that it plays in human development, social interaction, and personality.

This book presents many of these new advances and helps show their practical implications for daily life.

How could it be possible that something as important as personal memory was not a primary focus of study in psychology for most of the previous century? I have provided a detailed response to this question elsewhere (Singer and Salovey 1993), but the brief answer is that there were two major movements in twentieth-century psychology that argued against the study of the familiar stories that we tell about our life experiences. The first movement, psychoanalysis, argued that we do not really know ourselves; the truth to our personality lies beneath the surface in the murky depths of the unconscious. The second movement, behaviorism, proposed that a rigorous science of human nature could not rely on subjective experience, but required measurement limited to stimuli and responses that could be objectively observed and recorded. Caught in the crossfire of these two powerful forces in psychology was the deceptively simple idea that what people thought about themselves and their past experiences might indeed provide great insight into their desires, goals, emotions, and struggles to find personal meaning.

By the end of the twentieth century, the dominant schools of psychoanalysis and behaviorism had given way to the information age, and psychology embraced the metaphor of the brain as a complex and intricate computer. This cognitive revolution, which is increasingly linked to advances in neuroscience, reopened interest in how we take in and make sense of important information in our lives. Psychology turned its lens both to the hardware of the brain—the anatomical and biochemical substrates of thought—and the software—the ways in which we organize information and connect that information to emotion and behavior.

Despite this renewed willingness to take conscious thought seriously, cognitive psychologists were originally absorbed by the study of the "process" of memory rather than its content. With the computer as their model, they performed decades of experiments in controlled laboratory conditions examining how individuals "encoded," "stored," and "retrieved" lists of words or phrases that had little relevance to individuals' actual lives.

Finally, in 1978 Ulrich Neisser, one of the founders of cognitive psychology, wrote a scathing critique of his own field, stating that memory researchers were failing to answer the important questions about how memory works in real life. In fact, he argued that one could offer the theorem that If X is an interesting or socially significant aspect of memory, then psychologists have hardly ever studied X (Neisser 1982, 4).

Along with Neisser, other memory researchers including Eugene Winograd, David Rubin, Marigold Linton, John Robinson, and Martin Conway began to turn their attention to what they called at various times *real-world memory*, *everyday memory*, *autobiographical memory*, and *personal memory*. This new movement in memory psychology opened the way for fascinating studies of people's memories. These researchers examined touchstone events in people's lives (called *flashbulb memories* due to their vividness and amount of detail), such as when people heard the news of President Kennedy's assassination or the crash of the Challenger space shuttle. They studied the accuracy and content of John Dean's memory by examining his testimony during the Watergate hearings that led to President Nixon's resignation. (More recently, memory researchers turned their attention to people's memories for the events of 9/11/2001 in New York City and Washington, D.C.)

New research also looked at how people organized their personal memories and the role that emotion played in the ability to recall memories. Some memory researchers turned to questions of traumatic memories. Did some people truly repress them as Freud had hypothesized? Was there really such a thing as a "recovered memory"? Others examined the differences in the memories of children compared to adults, while others began investigations of memory in the elderly.

At the same time that this new explosion of research on socially relevant and personally significant memories was gaining its full force, revolutionary advances in brain science were leading to remarkable discoveries about the role of different brain structures and chemicals in the creation, retention, and retrieval of memories. The work of Endel Tulving at the University of Toronto and Daniel Schachter at Harvard University, among many other researchers, began to reveal how the brain coordinated a variety of memory systems that respectively handled memory for specific events, abstract concepts, sensory images, and well-rehearsed motor routines, such as hitting a golf ball or playing the piano. Lesions or injury in different sites of the brain could lead to disruptions in one or more of these systems. Studies of patients with brain damage or unusual memory disorders (see chapter 1) revealed even more information about the actual mechanics of personal memory. In the quarter century since Neisser's fateful challenge, memory research could no longer be considered too detached or unconcerned with the real memories of real people.

The Role of Memory in Personality and Therapy

Increasingly, clinical psychologists and psychotherapists have been able to draw on this memory research to gain insights into the memories that their patients share with them. At the same time, researchers in the fields of personality and social psychology have placed growing importance on the role that memory plays in emotions, attitudes, self-concept, and interpersonal interactions. All of this research suggests that the kinds of memories we recall and how we think about our memories play a central role in understanding ourselves, as well as the world around us.

In over twenty years of work as a clinical psychologist and researcher in the area of memory and personality, I have devoted myself to exploring how this burgeoning literature on personal memory can be applied to the most basic questions of identity, mental health, and optimal adjustment. In particular, I have studied how certain types of personal memories, "self-defining memories," as discussed in chapter 1, play a critical role in self-understanding, control of emotion, and motivation.

In addition to these laboratory studies of memory, I have worked with patients in individual, couples, and family therapy over the same period of time. In my work as a therapist, a major focus of my efforts has been to help my patients identify the personal memories that capture their most significant themes and conflicts. In many of my books and articles, I have presented case studies of individuals who use their personal memories as the foundations of their self-understanding and motivation to change. In partnership with these patients, I have helped to identify the self-defeating patterns or unexpected triumphs that emerge from their memories' imagery and plotlines. In work with couples, I have assisted partners in targeting shared memories that either divide them or bring them closer. Imagery exercises and role-playing have highlighted the emotional impact of these memories. They have often served as catalysts to aid the couple in achieving a healthier relationship.

The findings from my own research and clinical work, along with those of other researchers who share a similar interest in the power of personal memory, provide the foundation for this book. They guide the recommendations and exercises that will help you to gain greater control over your own personal memories in order to improve your self-understanding and change your life.

INVITATION TO BEGIN

With this overview under your belt, you are ready to start. Find a quiet place, turn off the cell phone, get the children to bed, and break out your pen and fresh pages of your memory journal. You are about to begin a journey into a world that is filled with millions of points of light. Yet each of those bursts of radiance is not a star, but the fire of an event long past now rekindled on your mind's dark screen. Illuminated, each image is a potential source of energy to propel you forward in your life.

1

Personal Memory and Self-Defining Memories

How does personal memory work? In this chapter, I share some of the major findings from the new science of personal memory and help you think about its relevance to your own memory. After reviewing some general principles of personal memory, I zero in on the memories most relevant to self-understanding and growth—self-defining memories. Once you master the five key elements of these memories, you will be ready to learn a method for identifying these memories in your own life.

WHAT IS PERSONAL MEMORY?

Personal memory is memory for the events that you have experienced firsthand. It is not memory for facts that you have learned or lists that you have studied. It is not memory for verb endings, parking spaces, or names you have heard at social gatherings. Personal memory is memory about sitting on your grandfather's lap, taking the bus your first day of school, seeing a lion at the zoo, or getting candy at the corner store.

Personal memory is the collection of events that make up your unique past and help to orient you about who you are and where you have come from. For all these reasons, the study of this kind of memory has the greatest relevance for understanding personality and what makes one person different from another.

Psychologists, psychiatrists and neuroscientists are making remarkable advances in understanding the biological substrates of memory. Using imaging techniques and EEG (electroencephalogram) recordings of the electrical activity in the brain, we have been able to track the flow of activity through the brain as you search for, retrieve, and then imagine a memory of a past event from your life. Martin Conway and his colleagues in England performed an ingenious series of studies with EEG recordings that demonstrated a three-stage process of memory retrieval in the brain. Conway, Pleydell-Pearce, and White-cross (2001) created an experiment to trace slow cortical potentials (essentially spikes in the electrical activity of the brain) when individuals use a cue word to find a memory, then hold and concentrate on this specific memory, and finally let go of the recalled experience. Using a computer screen, they had participants view a cue word to spark a memory related to that word (for example, home, knife, sadness), and then pull a lever to indicate that they had begun to search for the memory. Once they signaled they had found the memory, a new cue on the screen would tell the participants to keep the memory in mind and focus on its image. After this imaging period, another signal would tell the participants to let go of the memory image and rest before the next word was presented.

These experiments revealed a consistent pattern of electrical activity in different parts of the brain as participants searched for, retrieved, and then concentrated on their memories. During the search period, as people were sorting through their different possible memories, the left frontal areas of the brain, the areas associated with the most abstract kinds of thought, showed the most activity. Once participants settled on the memory, an area more toward the middle of the brain, the anterior temporal lobe, started to show more action. This area is associated with emotional responses and sequences of motor activity. Finally, as participants focused on the memory and reexperienced its events, the right hemisphere of the brain and portions toward the back of the brain—the posterior temporal and occipital areas— displayed activity. These areas are linked to both visual imagery and emotion.

Conway has used these experiments and other laboratory research to build an understanding of personal memory that is organized at three levels of a hierarchy (not unlike a filing system you might use at your office or home). When we try to find a personal memory from our lives, we start with very abstract or general categories—what he calls *lifetime periods.*

These lifetime periods are overarching categories like the early years of a marriage, graduate school, or a period of financial hardship. They are like the big drawers in the file cabinet. You can divide up your life in different ways and each period can consist of longer or shorter stretches of time. Since these lifetime periods contain many different memories that are all linked by a shared time frame and topic, it makes sense that the front part of the brain that handles abstract associations and generalizations would be most active when they are in use.

The next level of personal memory is what Conway calls *general events.* General events are categories of events that make up relatively brief time periods (a week, a day, a few hours) and are organized by a common theme (such as first-time experiences, academic successes, dating experiences, surprise parties, favorite vacations). General events are like the folders inside the drawer of a particular lifetime period. Once you identify a lifetime period (college days), you can leaf through the folder of dating experiences in order to find a particular one that you might want to remember. The reason that these general events folders are linked to the middle parts of the brain involved in emotion and action is that often we organize our familiar activities around goals. As we shall see, getting or not getting our goals is linked closely to the kind and strength of emotion we feel in our lives.

Finally, when we reach for a specific sheet of paper from the general events folder of our memory, we are grabbing at what Conway calls *event-specific knowledge.* Event-specific knowledge is the portion of personal memory that consists of specific images associated with a unique event in your life. Starting from college days, moving to dating experiences, you can now select the specific blind date in your sophomore year that led to a romance that lasted for the next two years. You can remember the exact spring night of the date, see the restaurant where you first met, and recall the excited conversation with your roommate about the awesome time you had that evening. These sensory images help to explain why the occipital lobe, which is linked to the visual pathway of the brain, is so active during this phase of memory retrieval.

These three levels—lifetime periods, general events, and event-specific knowledge—all combine to yield a rich and meaningful personal memory. For this process to work effectively, the brain must achieve the proper balance between drawing on specific imagery based on past events and abstract knowledge we have built up about our lives, goals, and preferences—what Conway and I have called the *long-term self* (Conway, Singer, and Tagini 2004).

To achieve this balance, personal memory needs to be a very effective filing system. If we filed every experience from our lives, we would have cabinets that stretched for football fields and folders that could fill several stadiums. On the other hand, if we discarded experience after experience and never paused to put some of them in their proper drawer and folder, we would have little sense of continuity or meaning in our lives.

> **Effective personal memory, then, is a selection process that requires the ability to forget as well as remember personal events from your life.**

Contemporary researchers tend to agree that the key to how the brain succeeds in this selection process is the linkage of memory to ongoing goals in your life. As we talk about self-defining memories, we will spell out the exact nature of this linkage. For now, let's consider what would happen if your brain failed in this selection process. First, let's consider individuals who are unable to be selective in what they forget. Then we'll turn to individuals who cannot control what they remember. These examples should make very clear the critical importance of personal memory in our lives.

Remembering to Forget

Imagine if you made a lasting memory of every event in your daily life. What if every time you adjusted the blinds in your office or said, "Hi, how are you?" on your way to a meeting it became a distinct memory lodged in your brain. Imagine having to recall every time you put out the garbage, walked the dog, or poured a cup of coffee. In his story "Funes, His Memory," the great Argentine writer Jorge Luis Borges considers exactly this problem. We meet Ireneo Funes, a man who had suffered a fall from a horse and then found that he had lost all capacity to forget any experience past or present. Confined to his bed, he literally remembered everything:

> The truth was, Funes remembered not only every leaf of every tree in every patch of forest, but every time he had perceived or imagined the leaf. He resolved to reduce every one of his past days to seventy thousand recollections. . . . Two considerations dissuaded him; the realization that the task was interminable, and the realization that it was point-less. He saw by the time he died he would still have not finished classifying . . . his childhood. (Borges 1998, 136)

Overwhelmed and aging prematurely, Funes died at age twenty-one of pulmonary congestion, drowned by the flood of his own recollections. What this story illustrates is that memory is not simply a passive recorder, taking in each and every moment that occurs. Over our lifetimes, memory is a sifting process that retains the critical nuggets of our daily experiences. The trivial and mundane events, the ones that are repeated and routine, are either forgotten or blended into general events that lack the immediacy of specific memories.

Moving from fiction to an actual case, the celebrated Russian neurologist Alexander Luria (1982) studied an individual, S. V. Shereshevski, known in the literature as S., who was a renowned mnemonist (an individual with unusual powers of memory recall). S. could remember thousands of numbers at a time or hundreds of random objects. His powers of memory were almost limitless, but they were all based on his capacity to create a visual image of the item he was remembering. For him, memory was no harder than the act of seeing. However, despite his ability to remember everything, he strug-gled to draw any generalizations or abstractions from his expansive field of memories. He could only see the tree that each memory presented, and never the forests to which they belonged. He could remember event-specific knowledge, but could never connect it to more general events or to the major periods of his life.

These examples illustrate that we must be able both to be selec-tive about our personal memories and to make meaningful connections among the memories that we retain. For memories to matter in our lives, we must see how they relate to each other and to the larger goals, plans, or wishes of our lives. The ability to find these connections necessarily relies on our ability to put on the brakes and see that that some memories are irrelevant to important themes in our lives. We have to be just as good at saying, "That does not matter," as we are at tagging a memory for its importance.

Forgetting to Remember

Having stated the importance of forgetting for identifying the memories that matter, let's now consider the more obvious problem of not being able to remember anything at all. What would it be like if every time your friend entered the room you needed to be reintroduced to her? Or if you could not remember the topic of a conversation that had taken place only a few minutes before? Or if you could not recall where you were currently living or how you had ended up living there? This is the problem of not being able to retain any specific memories.

One of the most famous patients in the annals of psychology had exactly this problem. Called H.M. to protect his anonymity, he was a bright young man of twenty-seven years of age who suffered from increasingly powerful epileptic seizures. In 1953, the surgeon William Scoville operated on his temporal lobes (located in the lower middle region of his brain), removing a fist-size section that included structures called the hippocampus and amygdala. The rationale behind the surgery at the time was that the electrical activity that set off seizures had been traced to this temporal lobe location, and if you could disrupt this circuit, it would stop the spread of activity to the rest of the brain.

Although the seizures subsided, H.M. displayed a remarkable change in memory that no one had anticipated. He suffered from two major forms of memory problems. First, although he could remember events from his life up to age sixteen, he could not remember any events between then and the age of twenty-seven, which was his age at the time of the surgery.

More concerning, and what has led to H.M.'s enduring fame in memory research is that he also lost the capacity to create any new memories. In other words, he rapidly forgot any recent experiences that occurred in his life and consequently could no longer learn anything new. He would need to be introduced to his doctors every day. He could not accumulate any sense of the passage of time or events of history. He was stuck in a period in which Truman was president and World War II had recently ended. Each time he learned that his mother had died, he would again register the shock and pain of this news.

He lived this way for over forty years and patiently endured, with reasonably good humor, literally hundreds of studies of his memory functioning. As a living laboratory, H.M. helped to teach researchers the critical importance of the hippocampus, the seahorse-shaped portion of the midbrain or temporal region that plays a crucial function in the conversion of new information into stored long-term memories.

Besides teaching us about the linkages between portions of the brain and the different components of memory, H.M.'s tragic situation led many researchers to speculate about the relationship of memory to the self. If H.M. could not turn the present into the past, could not retain knowledge about the life he was currently living or remember the hopes or dreams he had envisioned in the previous day (or even the previous hour), if he lived in perpetual confusion and in a decade frozen in his youth, to what extent could we say that he continued to be a full person or retain a meaningful concept of self?

In a similar vein, think of the devastation to the self-concept that the over ten million Alzheimer's patients in this country must suffer. Imagine slowly losing familiarity with the objects, places, and finally people that you have known all your life. Imagine how this struggle to make sense of an intimate world that has suddenly become alien can disorient individuals from every bit of trusted reality and conviction of certainty that they have possessed. In his book on the Alzheimer epidemic, David Shenk (2003, 10) cites the words of one sufferer from Alzheimer's:

> The other day I was all confused in the street for a split second. I had to ask somebody where I was and I realized the magnitude of this disease. . . . It is a whole structure in which windows fall out, and then suddenly before you know it, the façade breaks apart.
>
> This is the worst thing that can happen to a thinking person. You can feel yourself, your whole inside and outside, break down.
>
> —M. New York, New York

The examples of H.M. and Alzheimer's patients convey powerfully that it is hard to imagine a sense of self or identity without an effective memory. The personality psychologist Dan McAdams has argued persuasively that our identity is no more or less than the life story we construct from the memories of our lives. As we move from adolescence to adulthood, we rely on memories to forge a meaningful story of who we are, based on a knowledge of our past experiences. This life story of identity draws on memories of our most important relationships, achievements, traditions, and first experiences. It helps us identify the most important heroes and villains, confidants and betrayers—the people who have made us who we are. It reminds us of the familiar strategies for success and the pitfalls that lead to frustration. Our ability to draw on these memories and connect them to our life stories provides us with a sense of continuity and purpose in our lives. With memory, our life is a vivid movie screen with a constant flow of images moving before our inner eye. Without memory or with a failing memory, there is only a gray screen and a looming darkness.

Our very sense of living a full human life is tied up with our capacity for effective personal memory. We must forget memories in order to extract meaningful generalizations from our experiences, but we also must retain memories if we ever hope to have a stable sense of identity and experience continuity across our lives.

We must be able to forget and remember—to let go of the less important events while at the same time retaining the critical ones that let us know who we are and what we want to be.

Now that we have laid out a basic framework of personal memory, we can turn to the question of how to identify the most important of these personal memories. Continuing our file folder metaphor of personal memory, there are some sheets within your file cabinet that have been flagged with red dots. These particular sheets of paper represent the most important or significant information in your whole filing system. Among the thousands of personal memories that you have retained, how might we proceed to uncover the very ones that matter most—your self-defining memories?

SELF-DEFINING MEMORIES AND BUBBE PSYCHOLOGY

In psychology, when a researcher presents a finding based on extensive data collection that seems intuitive or commonsensical (such as, attractive people tend to be more popular), fellow researchers may dismiss the work by calling it "bubbe psychology." In other words, it's something that your grandmother could have told you without wasting all that time in the laboratory (*bubbe* is the Yiddish world for "grandmother"). The story of self-defining memories begins with another kind of grandmother psychology—one that involves an actual grandmother.

However, before we get to the grandmother we have to start in a research laboratory at Yale University. Many years ago when I was a first-year graduate student, I was studying the physiological patterns of different emotional states. I used electrodes to measure changes in brain activity, heart rate, and blood pressure. In order to measure how the body might respond differently to anger versus sadness, or fear versus joy, I had to induce very strong emotions in my study participants. The simplest and most effective way to do this was to ask them to recall experiences from their lives that had made them feel passionately (in some of our studies I used acting students who were particularly good at connecting to their past experiences and bringing up current feelings). As a young graduate student, I became fascinated by the power of these recalled experiences to affect the participants' minds and bodies. We could see dramatic differences in their heart rate and blood pressure, and we made sure to have a tissue box on hand for their tears. In time I became more entranced by the fact their memories could provoke these emotions than by the bodily patterns produced by their emotional states. This fascination led me to ask a very simple question that I have studied ever since:

Why do some memories more than others have the capacity, years after the original event has occurred, to continue to evoke tears or laughter, dismay or joy?

At the same time that I was beginning to define this research question, I was also participating in another important activity of my life—calling my grandmother every Sunday night. My grandmother at that time had recently lost her husband of over fifty years and lived alone in a small apartment in Brighton Beach, Brooklyn. As a typical Jewish grandmother, Yetta doted on her grandchildren and her day was transformed by a simple phone call from one of them. As these calls continued over the years, I began to notice a repetitive pattern in the stories she would share with me. Something in our conversation would set her off and the jukebox of her memory would start to whir and then play one of the familiar and favorite stories of her life as a little girl. I came to think of these as "Little Yetta" stories and knew a good half dozen of them by heart. Each story shared a similar theme of a little girl of considerable promise being overlooked or neglected, but ultimately vindicated and celebrated for her gifts by a powerful authority figure. In one memory, it was the school principal who recognized her ability to read when her own teacher had not. In another, it was Eleanor Roosevelt (in the days when Franklin was still just a congressman in New York City) visiting Little Yetta's community center and acknowledging her singing voice. In another, a local official awarded Yetta a prize for her patriotic essay. No matter who the major characters were and the exact details of the plot, each memory ended with delighted laughter and pride in her voice.

What struck me at the time was the parallel to the participants in my blood pressure studies of emotion—my grandmother experienced such strong emotion each and every time from telling her memories. But why did these particular memories cause this effect? What gave these memories their power? What made them the memories that mattered most to her?

To answer this question, I tried to think about what place these memories held in my grandmother's life. Forced to flee from persecution in the waning days of the Austro-Hungarian empire, my grandmother's family came to the United States at the turn of the twentieth century. Although her older brothers had received university education in Europe, she was the only one of the younger siblings to graduate high school in the United States. Having demonstrated great intellectual promise, she was admitted to Hunter College in New York City. However, due to the events of World War I, she was forced to withdraw after one year. The United States had just entered the war and her older brother was in danger of being drafted. With a daughter in college, the family could not make a convincing argument to the draft board that her brother was needed to help provide for the family. The choice was clear—Yetta had to stop college.

In her subsequent years of marriage and raising a family of two children, Yetta never resumed her education, but she put every fiber of her being into the intellectual progress of her son and daughter. Both children went on to earn advanced degrees and one of them (my father) became a professor at an Ivy League university. Considering these details puts the Little Yetta memories in a very meaningful light. These memories contain the theme of vindication and recognition for her personal accomplishments that remained unrealized in Yetta's actual life. The power of these memories is that they are linked to a central goal for Yetta—the desire to be valued for her own intellectual and artistic gifts, to be the Little Yetta who finally comes to the head of the class.

In seeing the connection between the emotional responses of my participants and Yetta's memories, I had the beginning of a possible answer to the question of why certain memories matter so much:

**Certain memories keep their emotional power
because they are linked to goals and desires that
are still most important in our lives.**

Until the day my grandmother died, she esteemed learning and education as almost sacred activities. Memories that reflected what she continued to love had the power to move her. They were the ones that returned with increasing frequency to her mind as the other aspects of her life were slowly winnowed away by the frailties of age.

This realization thrilled me with the force of a scientific discovery. For any person, there might be a set of special memories, their particular photo album of well-thumbed images that reflect their life's most critical and pressing desires. To learn about these memories and to see the connections among them might reveal something critical about that person. It might be a window into a genuine understanding of what mattered most to them.

I was off and running. What followed was a Ph.D. dissertation, numerous articles and chapters, four books, and more than twenty years of fascination with people's most significant memories. A few years after I began the study of these personal memories, I was driving cross-country with my wife. We were sitting on a rock ledge, taking in a beautiful vista at Arches National Park in Utah. I was explaining to her that although I had begun to publish my research, I did not feel like I had found a way to describe the memories I studied. When I told people that I did research on memory, they would ask me why they could not remember the names of people that they had just met or where they had parked their car after an afternoon of shopping. To avoid this kind of confusion, I needed a way to convey the essence of these special personal memories that I had begun to collect. And then the phrase "self-defining memories" came to me and it seemed to capture perfectly the kind of memory I had identified.

I have used this term ever since in both my research and clinical work. Increasingly, other researchers in psychology have adopted this

> **Self-defining memories are those memories that help you to define most clearly how you see yourself and that help explain who you are to another person.**

phrase and studies have been conducted or are underway all around the globe, including the United Kingdom, Spain, Mexico, the Netherlands, Bulgaria, Canada, and Australia. These researchers are studying a variety of questions related to the role of self-defining memories in mental and physical health, personality, and social relationships. I shall touch on much of this work in the chapters ahead, but for right now my current goal is to help you know exactly what self-defining memories are and how you can locate them in your own life.

WHAT ARE SELF-DEFINING MEMORIES?

Just for a moment think of your memory as a digital camera that takes thousands and thousands of photos each day. Imagine that at the end of the day you are like any tourist who has returned from a trip and now must sort through the countless number of shots. No one is going to want to see a hundred photos of the same mountaintop or all those shots where you cut off someone's head or had your strap in front of the lens. So you delete the fuzzy photos and the repeats. Then you realize no one is going to want to see the photo of the person that you met briefly at the visitor's center and who shared a few jokes with you. So you put that photo and many other similar, less important ones in a file for safekeeping (but probably not one to which you are likely to return very often, if at all). Finally, you have boiled down the countless shots to the most meaningful collection of photos and it's these few that you insert into your PowerPoint display or electronic photo album.

Over the weeks, months, and years, these images, to which you return repeatedly, become your touchstone for remembering this past experience. Now imagine that, as time goes on, you accumulate more and more of these photo collections filled with meaningful images. Imagine, too, that with the power of PhotoShop or some other editor you can rearrange their order, zoom in on a person or an object, heighten the contrast or colors, or even choose to delete more of the photos that you had originally saved. As your life goes on and your goals and desires endure or change, you can sort through, select, or edit the images from the collections that you have created.

The process I am describing is roughly equivalent to the process of creating, preserving, and recalling your most important self-defining memories. These memories are the selective records of the most important events in your life. However, they are not simple reproductions of those events with each detail set in stone, never to change.

The actual content, form, and emotional power of your self-defining memories can change subtly or dramatically over the course of your life. What causes the memories to change is that your interests, desires, and goals change. As you change where you seek to go in the future, the contribution of past experiences to that new direction becomes more or less important.

If the memories that matter most to you can change, how do we know that any particular memory is self-defining? Our research has determined that self-defining memories always retain the five following elements:

1. Emotional intensity

2. Vividness

3. Repeated recall

4. Connections to similar memories

5. Focus on lasting goals or unresolved conflicts

In the sections that follow, try to begin to zero in on some memories from your own life that match each of these elements. Once I have explained them all, I describe the specific exercise that individuals in our research studies and my therapeutic work use to find their own particular self-defining memories. You will then be ready to try it yourself.

Emotional Intensity

For a memory to be self-defining, it must take hold of your feelings. When you recall this memory, your pulse should quicken or shivers should start; the hair on the back of your neck should rise or your face should flush a crimson tone. If it can't bring a strong rush of pleasure, a smile to your lips, or a lump in your throat, then most likely there is another memory of greater power that has replaced this memory's importance in your life. Self-defining memories touch too close to the heart to be taken lightly.

Self-defining memories are just as likely to generate painful feelings upon their recall as they are positive ones. Consider the emotional impact of this memory on this middle-aged woman who participated in one of our research projects:

> *When I was eight, I brought an African-American classmate from school home with me. My father was very pleasant the whole time she visited; he gave us milk and cookies and talked with us. After my friend left, he told me that I should never bring that type of person to his house again and spanked me. I was horrified. The problem is that I still feel terrified when I think of this memory and somehow I have never been able to be friends with a person of color again.*

Researchers have indeed verified that memories that are more emotional are remembered better and recalled faster. In addition, your mood can often influence the memories that you recall. We will cover issues of mood and memory in depth in chapter 4, but the key point here is that you are more likely to recall memories that match your current mood and it often requires more mental effort to find those memories that do not match your current emotional state. This is good news if you are generally a person who stays in good moods, but it may present a problem if you are someone who is inclined to negative moods. If you are prone to depression, it will take even more work for you to find the right memory to counteract your blues.

A last point to mention, which leads us to our next key element, is that memories that are more emotionally powerful are also more vivid—they are easier to visualize and reexperience in your mind's eye.

Vividness

From William James on, many psychologists have described our ongoing thoughts, fantasies, daydreams, memories, worries, and concerns as a stream of consciousness. Our waking minds are constantly responding to a never-ending flow of information, coming not just from the world outside our bodies, but also from our own restless thoughts.

Researchers who have studied daydreaming have found that when we engage in active daydreaming, we show reduced eye movement, less ability to follow moving objects, and slower reaction time to flashing lights or noises. We are literally watching the world inside us while we let go of our focus on the sensory world around us. In this theater of our mind, memories, fantasies, and even recent dreams are in a constant competition for attention, battling for center stage with shopping lists, recent conversations, and work issues—what the psychologist Eric Klinger (1999) calls "current concerns."

The thoughts that evoke the strongest images are the likely winners in this contest. When they come to mind, they make you feel like you are living in that image's moment rather than the present one. For example, here's the well-known young adult author Lauraine Snellings's depiction of a young girl's immersion in her dream of being a future Olympian:

> She, thirteen-year-old DJ Randall—well, fourteen minus twenty-one days—would hear the roar of the crowd as she and her mount triumphantly finished the cross-country course. When DJ closed her eyes again, she could almost feel the horse beneath her, the thrust of its powerful haunches sending them flying easily over the jumps. She could hear the cheers of the crowd, smell and taste the victory. (Snellings 1995, 1)

Only her best friend's insistent calling from the bottom of the stairs can pull DJ out of her reverie.

Not only visions of the future but memories of past events share the power to stop time and fill our senses from their images. The capacity to be overwhelmed by these visions is not simply a form of child's play, but remains a vital part of consciousness across all stages of life. The French novelist Marcel Proust, who wrote a seven-volume exploration of the role of memory in life and art (*Remembrance of Things Past*) describes being overtaken by a memory with the same intensity as any vivid daydream:

> These resurrections of the past are so complete that they do not merely oblige our eyes to become oblivious to the room before them . . . they also force our nostrils to inhale the air of places which are . . . far remote [and] . . . compel our entire being to believe itself surrounded by them. (Proust 1932, 201)

Yet in imagining the future or reexperiencing an event from the past, it is important to ask if these vivid images are simply reproductions of actual life. The answer is no, and the reason why tells us something important about self-defining memories. The images our fantasies and memories create are not just snapshots that capture reality as it once was or is likely to be. The vivid images that engage our stream of ongoing thought contain something beyond any realistic depiction. They are illuminated by our desires and also at times by our sorrows. In a sense their vividness is due to a quality of symbolism—their iconic power in our mind makes them larger and more defined than actual events from our life. In the young girl's dream of glory, all eyes are on her and she is literally at the center of the world. For Proust, the artistic beauty of the past is its ineffable mystery. It contains a depth that no moment of the present can match—"the only true paradise is the paradise we have lost" (p. 195).

The vivid images created by self-defining memories are like the statues or frescoes in a cathedral. In immediate and emotionally evocative symbols, they highlight for us what matters most. In their intensity and clarity, they just about re-create the world, but then take it one step further.

Repetition

Self-defining memories are not like those casual acquaintances that enter your life on rare occasions, perhaps at a college reunion or a yearly picnic, and then recede to the far reaches of your life. They are more like family members, loved or dreaded, who call or appear on a regular basis, and whose contact, depending on your feelings toward them, provokes a rush of pleasure or a knot in the stomach.

For example, my colleagues and I (Singer et al. 2002) collected self-defining memories from students who had experienced significant challenges during recent summer internship experiences. The students not only rated these memories as very important to them, but also indicated that they had thought about them on average between once a week and once a month since the experiences had occurred. Some students had thought about them almost every day. When looking at how they wrote about these memories, we found that students often commented, "Whenever I am down, I will think of that memory . . . and it will cheer me up" or "Before a big game [performance/test/ meeting], I will recall that memory and it will make a big difference in my attitude." This same process also worked in a negative or avoidant way, as when the students wrote, "Every time I try to make peace with my dad, I can't help but recall how he was not there for me this summer" or "Each time I try to overcome my fear, I remember the time that I . . ."

Why do these students and the rest of us draw on self-defining memories with such frequency? One reason may be the classic learning principle of facilitation. Once a set of associations is learned, the brain is primed to activate this pattern of connections in the brain. Each new activation only reinforces the relationship between the items or concepts that you have linked together.

We can easily see this phenomenon when you slip and call someone by the wrong name (let's say "Chris" instead of "Charles"). The next time you see Charles, your brain revives the recent association that you created between the sight of him and the name "Chris." Before you know it, you blurt out "Chris" again; and then, even worse, this second mistake only further strengthens the errant association. Ultimately, it takes a conscious effort and some forced rehearsal (repeating "Charles—Charles—Charles" right before you see him) to break the pattern.

The same thing is clearly taking place with the tendency of your mind to revive self-defining memories. A memory that you might have of a successful recital comes into your mind when you go to practice a new piece of music. The pleasant feelings of success that this memory revives are likely to reinforce this association and soon it becomes a familiar companion to the start of a practice session.

However, repetition of self-defining memories goes beyond just a property of learning. There are also motivational factors that play a role in reviving these memories on a frequent basis. As David Pillemer (1998) recounts in his book on personal memories, *Momentous Events, Vivid Memories*, individuals may repetitively recall memories to remind them of what they want, but also to warn them of the consequences of a negative outcome. He cites Michael Jordan's remarkable but true memory of being cut from a varsity basketball team in his sophomore year of high school. Jordan recalled:

> It was embarrassing, not making that team. They posted the roster and it was there for a long, long time without my name on it. I remember being mad too, because there was a guy who made it that really wasn't as good as me. . . .

> Whenever I was working out and got tired and figured
> I ought to stop, I'd close my eyes and see that list . . . , and
> that usually got me going again. (Pillemer 1998, 41)

The repetition of particular memories may also have a nostalgic rather than a motivating role. Individuals may frequently return to a memory not because it will guide them in future action, but simply because it revives for them something that they experienced in the past and feel that they cannot have again. We are all familiar with former athletes who live in the glory days depicted in Bruce Springsteen's song of the same name. We have encountered or read about the television celebrity who appears in shopping malls, sustained by loyal fans of his long-cancelled series. We may dismiss these individuals for their "wallowing" in the past, but in truth all of us look for solace from recollections of better moments in our lives. How comforting it is to recall a family holiday from childhood when life was no more complicated than deciding whether to open presents before or after breakfast!

There is yet another reason for why we return repeatedly to the same memories, but it has to do with how we respond to the deepest conflicts in our personality. I will wait to discuss this particular aspect of repetition when we turn to the role of conflict in self-defining memories.

Connections to Similar Memories

Another essential feature of my grandmother's Little Yetta stories was their similarity. I cannot say for sure how much she had taken different experiences and merged them over the years or whether she indeed had had many experiences with the same elements in common. The end result either way was that when Yetta started a story of her childhood exploits I knew that it would end on a similar triumphant note. In the 1970s, the personality psychologist Silvan Tomkins (1979) introduced script theory, a way of understanding how individuals organize the important experiences of their lives. His ideas helped me to make sense of how my grandmother might end up retelling a series of memories that overlapped in their plot and major themes. Tomkins suggested that human thought relies on basic units of scenes. Scenes consist of an action, an outcome, and an emotional response. A most basic scene can be, My mother holds me. I feel warm and smile.

As we grow from infancy to adulthood, we collect scenes and they gain in complexity of action, outcome, and emotion. A more complicated scene might be this one: My sister wins a prize. I am overlooked. I try to get attention, but my parents neglect me. I feel sad.

Tomkins's key insight was that personality emerges from the linking together of scenes that share similar plots, outcomes, and emotions. Ultimately, as in any process of thought, the bringing together of a number of similar entities creates a more general category or abstraction. Tomkins called this abstraction from a group of similar scenes a script. *Scripts* are the general themes that emerge from a set of connected scenes. They are like a mental blueprint.

Going back to our example of the scene in which the sister won a prize, we could imagine that her younger brother experienced several more of these painful episodes of neglect over the years of their growing up together (whether real or imagined we cannot say). This set of negative scenes might indeed have merged together to form a more abstract template of what life in his family was like. The script might go something like this: My sister is the center of the family. Her achievements get the spotlight. When I try to win attention, it never works. I am doomed to be in her shadow.

What are the implications of this script for this young man? Tomkins wrote that the script becomes a filter through which we recall past events and make sense of new experiences. For better or worse, these scripts can shape our perceptions and understanding of critical events and relationships in our lives. They are invaluable to us in situations where we feel overwhelmed by information or are unclear about how to respond. They tell us what to do and how to feel when we are caught without a response. The downside is that they may lead us to lump situations together too quickly and to misinterpret others' actions or responses.

A patient of mine who had repeatedly been humiliated by his parents as a child expected every encounter with someone intimate in his life to result in an episode of rejection and shame. He recounted several memories that shared a script in which he would follow a moment of connection with another person by an episode of withdrawal and shutting down. The resulting negative response from the person who had reached out to him served as confirmation that his efforts at intimacy will always yield rejection.

I experienced this pattern firsthand with this patient after a particularly emotional session in which he shared some painful insights and we felt a deepened bond in our relationship. The next meeting he came late and confessed that he had not given any thought to the therapy all week. When I asked him to talk about this statement, he announced that I was probably angry with him and for good reason. He then wondered if perhaps the whole therapy was a hopeless endeavor. Having felt too close to me last session, he now was following his script to push me away.

Over time we came to understand the way this script might take hold of him and how it would poison his efforts at being close with others. Knowing its pattern, we were able to detect moments when he started to follow its familiar path and then did our best to escape its negative routine.

Clearly, not all scripts play such a toxic role in our lives. In times of misfortune, a script that reassures us that there is indeed a spiritual force that can help us find meaning and purpose could be a vital asset in the face of disappointment. My grandmother's script that argued for the recognition of a child's talents may not have led to direct acknowledgment of her own gifts, but it certainly served as a motivating force to encourage my father toward similar goals.

There are many case studies that provide evidence for how these scripts operate in influencing our memories and actions. However, Demorest and Alexander (1992) also designed a clever study to illustrate the influence of scripts on individuals' thought processes. They asked a group of research participants to generate a series of important memories from their lives and then had trained raters identify the most dominant scripts in these memories. A month later these same participants returned to the laboratory and were asked to write some fictional stories. Raters then identified scripts drawn from the plotlines of these made-up stories. As script theory would predict, there was a striking overlap in each participant's scripts between the actual memories and the made-up stories. Evidently, we carry around certain ways of seeing the world and they surface not only in our memories of real events, but in our imaginary worlds as well.

Lasting Goals and Unresolved Conflicts

The final element that distinguishes self-defining memories from other memories is their relationship to the most central goals and conflicts of our lives. I will devote the next two chapters to these connections, but the key point here is the power of self-defining memories to alert us to what matters most in our life.

In the past few decades, many emotion researchers have pointed to the critical role of goals in emotion. The psychologist Ira Roseman provided evidence that emotions could be distinguished depending on goal outcomes (Roseman and Smith 2001; Roseman, Spindel, and Jose 1990). Joy is the product of getting the goal you desire, while disappointment emerges from a thwarted goal. Anger arises when someone or something blocks you from a goal you seek, and shame can be caused by your interference with another person's goals.

If emotions are so tightly linked to our important goals, then it stands to reason that a memory's emotional power depends on the relevance of the memory to the goals that matter most to you. This is in fact what my research and a number of other researchers have demonstrated over the past decade.

If you are someone who is very concerned about your relationships and making connections with other people, you are likely to have more emotional memories about relationships and intimacy. If you are someone concerned with achievement and getting ahead, your memories are more likely to contain emotional scenes filled with images of success and power. If you are someone concerned with making the world a better place and contributing to society, your memories are more likely to contain themes of helping others and social justice. And the more dominant any of these motives or goals are in your life, the more these memories will matter to you.

Of course, emotion about these memories works both ways. If you are an achievement-driven person, then a memory about a previous failure will continue to generate great sadness and disappointment in you. For some people (think of the Michael Jordan example), these memories about the nonattainment of their goals are the spurs to do better. Yet many of us may not have reached this place with these difficult memories. We may still recall memories that evoke strong emotion in us, but rather than move us ahead, they leave us stuck in that same negative place.

One of my patients, a salesman named Ray, describes his struggle to assert himself and how a childhood memory still plays a role in this battle:

> I am determined to speak up at work when my boss goes over
> the top and criticizes the whole department about some little

matter. We will have exceeded our sales figures and made him a ton of money, but he still gives us a ration of bull. Inside I can feel my heart pounding and my palms get all sweaty. Suddenly, I am right back at the kitchen table with my father poring over my geometry homework and telling me that my figures are sloppy and that I should use a better pencil. Once that memory takes over, the wind goes out of my sails and I feel like a defeated kid.

This memory is clearly self-defining for Ray, but it is linked more to an unresolved conflict than a positive goal. Ray wants to feel more powerful, but also wants to avoid being criticized by an authority figure who reminds him of his father. The emotional power of his memory is tied to the urgency of this continuing conflict in his life.

There is something very odd here on the surface. Why in the world would our minds keep recalling moments from our lives that only remind us of our disappointments, losses, or setbacks, especially when these reminders seem to bring us right back into the same quagmires and dilemmas?

What good is a memory that leaves us stuck in the quicksand of resentment or failure?

Sigmund Freud asked the very same question about nightmares. He had developed a theory of dreams that was based on the idea that all dreams expressed (usually in highly symbolic ways) the fulfillment of our wishes and secret desires. However, this theory, which helped to explain the convoluted logic of many dreams, did not help him to understand why individuals seemed to have recurring nightmares. This question particularly haunted him after he began to treat a number of World War I veterans who had traumatic recurring dreams about their war experiences (today we would diagnose these ex-soldiers with post-traumatic stress disorder, or PTSD).

In trying to answer this question, Freud wrote about what he called the "repetition compulsion" or the tendency of the person to return to images and to act out behaviors that reflected negative themes and conflicts in the personality. He suggested that one reason for this tendency might be that we are still trying to resolve these lingering conflicts and by bringing them back into our lives we create new opportunities to address them and conquer them once and for all. In other words, our minds revive them in order to give us a chance to master them.

To explain this idea, Freud described the child's game of peek-a-boo. The child takes a frightening recurring problem in her life—the disappearance from sight of important caregivers when they leave the room or go to sleep at night—and turns it into a game that is both at her initiative and under her control. Instead of feeling powerless over her parents' comings and goings, the child, by re-creating their appearances and disappearances under her own terms, gains a form of mastery over an upsetting event.

It may be that we continue to recall our painful memories in order to give ourselves opportunities to take control of these conflicts in our lives. It may not work the first time or even the hundredth time, but each time we revive the episode in our minds we also provide a window of opportunity for change and mastery. Much of my work as a therapist counts on exactly this idea—that my patients will bring these memories of conflict to the surface and then, using the techniques of psychotherapy, we can work toward better endings and greater control over these problems in their lives. In the next two chapters, I share many of these techniques from therapy so that you might put them to work to take control of the self-defining memories that express the unresolved conflicts in your life.

For now though, you have already taken a first step by learning how to identify the key features of self-defining memories. You are now ready for the next step—locating the specific memories that matter most in your own life.

IDENTIFYING YOUR SELF-DEFINING MEMORIES

For this exercise, it will be necessary to get out your memory journal and to find a quiet place where you will be able to do some careful reflection and writing. You are going to write down ten self-defining memories following the instructions that we have developed in numerous research studies over the last twenty years. All of the memories that you recall will need to be from at least one year ago or more. The reason for this time limit is similar to why we let good wines or cheeses age. By allowing time to pass since the remembered event, the memory is likely to take on more of the flavor of your personality; its relevance to the lasting goals and conflicts of your life will be more defined and articulated. Events that do not show this kind of deep connection will already have begun to fade in their impact. Some recent experiences that have an emotional impact for you now may feel very different to you in a year's time, if you remember them at all. To maximize your chances of locating the memories that will continue to matter most, we have always used this rule of a year's delay in our research.

For some of you it may seem daunting to have to write down so many important memories, but we have found that given enough time almost everyone we have asked can do this successfully. The reason we ask for such a large number is that this allows patterns across the memories to emerge. When you study the ten memories as a group, you begin to see the themes and scripts that link your memories together. Remember, you have many more self-defining memories than the ten you may end up choosing, but at least these ten can get you started on what can be a lifelong dialogue with this powerful source of self-understanding.

Are you feeling ready to begin?

EXERCISE I:
LISTING SELF-DEFINING MEMORIES

You are about to recall a special kind of personal memory called a self-defining memory. A self-defining memory has the following attributes:

- It is at least one year old.

- It is a memory from your life that you can remember very clearly and that still feels important to you even as you think about it.

- It is a memory about an important enduring theme, issue, or conflict from your life. It is a memory that helps explain who you are as an individual and might be the memory you would tell someone else if you wanted that person to understand you in a profound way.

- It is a memory linked to other similar memories that share the same theme or concern.

- It may be a memory that is positive or negative, or both, in how it makes you feel. The only important aspect is that it leads to strong feelings.

- It is a memory that you have thought about many times. It should be familiar to you like a picture you have studied or a song (happy or sad) you have learned by heart.

To understand best what a self-defining memory is, imagine you have just met someone you like very much and are going for a walk together. Each of you is very committed to helping the other get to know the "real you." You are not trying to play a role or to strike a pose. While, inevitably, we say things that present a picture of ourselves that might not be completely accurate, imagine that you are making every effort to be honest. In the course of the conversation, you describe a memory that you feel conveys powerfully how you have come to be the person you currently are. It is precisely this memory, which you tell the other person and simultaneously repeat to yourself, that constitutes a self-defining memory.

In our studies, our participants usually have had to write down their memories in one long session, but you don't need to approach your memories this way. You may want to look at your set of memories over the course of a few days or even a week to see if the group you have written down feels right to you. In one study we conducted, we had our participants return four different times over a month and each time asked them to review their memories with the option to change any or all of the memories they had chosen. We were pleased to see that they tended to keep the same group of memories with only a few modifications. In fact, on average, people changed only one or two memories of their group of ten. Still, it is entirely possible that your mood or life circumstances might affect the kinds of memories that emerge. This is perfectly all right because, as we mentioned earlier, when your goals change, the memories you experience as self-defining are likely to change too. You may keep the same self-defining memory but change what you emphasize or feel about it, or you may replace a memory with another one that is more connected to your current goals.

In choosing your ten most important self-defining memories, it may be helpful to think about some life domains or your own personal lifetime periods and then find the significant memories from these categories. For example, you might use the domains of family, relationships, work, and favorite activities to spur your recollections. Other individuals have found it useful to employ time periods from their lives, such as childhood, adolescence, early adulthood, and so on. You might also make explicit use of the lifetime periods that Conway has identified—for example, your college years, first job, first home, marriage before children, time in the military, and so on.

There is no right or wrong way to find your most important memories. The only thing that matters is that you feel that they are honest expressions of who you are and what matters most to you. As each memory comes to mind, write down a description of it in your journal, numbering each memory from one to ten. Try to write as clear and specific a description of the memory as you can. The more detail you include, the more likely the feeling and meaning that the memory holds for you will emerge.

Remember, my own research has found that retrieving these memories can be a very powerful emotional experience. It might bring tears, joy, or anger back with a force that you might not have anticipated. This is why it is important to give yourself some quiet time and space to do this. However, the very nature of self-defining memories is that they are often shared with other people, so do not hesitate to seek support or discuss them with others if you feel so inclined. You are taking a journey of self-understanding, but you need not do it alone or in ways that cause unnecessary discomfort. Family members, friends, counselors, or pastors are all there to help and serve as resources as you engage in this self-exploration.

It will be absolutely fascinating to see what you come up with. No two memories are ever identical and no two people's sets of memories are ever the same. To me, each set of self-defining memories is like a new poem or story unfolding. So go ahead and start your masterpiece.

EMOTIONAL RESPONSES TO YOUR MEMORIES

At this point, I am assuming that you have written down your ten memories and given yourself a chance to review them and settle on a list that you might keep for a while. If so, then we are ready to move forward with looking at them in a variety of ways. The first thing I would like you to do is to consider how each memory makes you feel *now* in recalling it. I emphasize *now* because, as I have already said, strong current feelings about the memory are the clue that this memory has retained its connection to your most important goals. The next exercise asks you to rate these emotions in order to understand better what you are feeling and what emotions are strongest for you. You might want to reread the description of each memory that you have written in your journal and then proceed with filling out the following rating sheet for each of your ten memories.

EXERCISE 2: RATING MEMORY EMOTIONS FOR EACH OF YOUR TEN MEMORIES

Using the rating scale below, go back and reread each memory. Then number a clean page in your journal from 1 to 10. Starting with Memory 1 in your journal and using the list below, choose the most powerful emotions that you feel when you think about this memory. Write down these emotions and rate them on a scale from 1 to 6 (1 being Not at All and 6 being Extremely). Then move on to Memory 2 and work your way down the column until you finish with Memory 10.

0   1   2   3   4   5   6

Not at All . . . Moderately . . . Extremely

Happy _____

Sad _____

Angry _____

Fearful _____

Surprised _____

Ashamed _____

Disgusted _____

Guilty _____

Interested _____

Embarrassed _____

Contemptful _____

Proud _____

Now that you have the ten memories in your journal and have given each memory its emotion rating, take some time to look over your list of memories and the emotions associated with them. What patterns do you see? Are your memories generally on the positive or negative side? Are they filled with pride or embarrassment, anger or sadness?

Are many memories about relationships, successes, failures, family moments? Do you see a repeating pattern across the memories that might constitute a script or an unresolved issue or conflict in your life? Do you see themes of overcoming adversity—an ability to bounce back or learn from disappointment?

CONCLUDING THOUGHTS

This chapter offered a picture of personal memory that is based on the need to both remember *and* forget events that take place in your life. Self-defining memories are particularly vivid memories that endure due to their relevance to your most important ongoing goals. The next chapter helps you to see the connection between the self-defining memories that you have listed and your personal goals. You will learn what these memories have to say about whether or not you are moving in the right direction to make those goals a reality.

2

Using Self-Defining Memories to Reach Your Goals

What do you want? Underneath all the work that I do as a therapist, I must inevitably tackle this bare-bones question with every person who enters my office and asks for help. However, this question is not simply for people in pain who are seeking counseling and guidance. It is the central question for every one of us. How should we direct our lives to maximize the feeling that we have lived well, that we have not wasted the precious opportunity of being alive? In this chapter I teach you a method for identifying the most pressing and important goals in your life. In particular, I ask you to focus on your *reach strivings*, a special type of goal that expresses what you most want, but that you also find the most difficult to attain. Once you have identified these important goals in your life, I illustrate how you can use your self-defining memories to bring you closer to their fulfillment.

WHAT DO WE REALLY WANT?

As adults, we often act like we know what we want. We get dressed in the morning and head out down the road in cars that speed us to our work (if we are not backed up in traffic), or we race around the house taking care of an endless "to-do" list. Our days zoom forward; we barely stop for lunch and, between children's swim practice, soccer, and orthodontist appointments, hardly pause for dinner. By nine o'clock, we turn to our partner and find him or her asleep with the television going or a book lying open. We tell ourselves that this pace of going full tilt on automatic pilot will end soon, that it is "just a phase," but then we look back and see that it has been five or ten years of a similar manic routine. Is this what we want? Is the life that we are currently leading bringing us closer to what we really want?

In this chapter you'll work through a set of exercises and techniques that cut through this whirlwind of activity and ask you to regroup and return to the most basic problems of living—what do you really want? What are the dreams that matter most to you? And is your current life bringing you closer to or further away from getting what you want? The key to answering these questions lies ironically in the past and the future more than in the present. What you are doing now is almost always a response to both what you have experienced in the past and what you are hoping to achieve in the years ahead. By understanding how you link your past and your future, you can reconsider and change what you are doing in the present. The tools for making these changes are your goals and your self-defining memories. You have already made a search through your past and found a set of your most significant memories. Now you will learn how to define your most important goals. With both memories and goals in hand, you can take the critical step of linking the two together. The ability to see and feel these connections will allow you to put your memories to work to attain the goals you most desire.

Getting to Your Most Important Goals

You may be thinking that the question What do I want? is too simplistic. Life is filled with so many demands, so many needs that compete for time and attention. How can you possibly boil down your complicated life into a straightforward statement of your desires and goals?

For many years I worked as the staff psychologist for an addiction agency that treats the most hard-core chronic substance abusers (discussed in my book, *Message in a Bottle: Stories of Men and Addiction*, Singer 1997). After years of self-destructive behaviors, these men and women would often reach an existential crisis. Having served time in jail or prison, endured multiple hospitalizations, lost jobs, marriages, and all their self-respect, they would describe themselves as being on their knees under the weight of their addiction and the suffering it had caused. For these addicted individuals who genuinely yearned for sobriety, three questions, framed so beautifully years ago by the psychiatrist William Glasser (2000), were like hammer blows to their hearts.

- What do you want?

- Is what you are doing right now getting you what you want?

- If not, what will?

Many individuals who successfully achieved sobriety and rebuilt their lives learned to use these questions as an incessant mantra throughout their daily lives. "If I want to stay sober, will stopping by my old neighborhood bar (even if I have a soda), really help me to achieve that?" "If I want to rebuild trust at work, will calling in sick on a Monday get me closer to my goal?" "If I sneak just one drink from time to time, will that allow me to see myself as an honest person who has let go of the lies and half-truths?" In my work with recovering alcoholic and drug-addicted individuals, I would often tell them how much I admired their courage for exactly this commitment to facing their goals and actions head-on.

How many of us in our so-called "normal" lives, in our business dealings or social gatherings, have the honesty to step back and scrutinize our actions in such a direct and naked way? In my work with people in recovery, I often refer to what I call the "pillow test." Can they at the end of the day lay their head on their pillow and say to themselves, "I have tried to live my life today honestly and in pursuit of the goals I most value. I may not have succeeded in every respect, but my actions took me in the right direction. If I can answer in this way, then I can put my head down on my pillow and be ready to take on the next day."

Over the years I have come to realize how this straightforward emphasis on defining and pursuing the goals you want in the most honest way possible extends far beyond my work with addicted individuals. I return to these three simple questions in therapy with troubled adolescents, individuals struggling with life decisions, and couples in marital therapy. So often the elemental simplicity of returning to the most basic concerns of your life cuts through all the layers of rationalizations, mistaken assumptions, and negative habits that block you from truly doing what is best for you.

Of course, if these questions are to work their magic, you must know what you want! The addicted person who has lost everything no longer has any ambiguity about what he or she wants. Like a foundry that has melted away all impurities to reveal the purest ore, the addiction has seared away all artifices, leaving the individual to see that sobriety is the only possible goal that will lead away from despair and death. For the person choosing a path of recovery, all the turns in the road lead one way—live one day at a time and commit not to use for that day. Each choice and action can be evaluated by the standard of how it helps or hinders that goal.

For the rest of us whose lives are entangled with multiple responsibilities, relationships, ambitions, and obligations, it may seem much harder to achieve this purity of purpose in defining and pursuing our goals. Yet the clearer and simpler we can make the driving concerns of our lives, the more likely we will be to define courses of action that will make these desires attainable.

In order to help you in this challenging undertaking, I provide you with a powerful method for identifying your most important personal goals. Developed by the psychologist Robert Emmons (1999) and backed by a series of research studies, the personal strivings assessment instrument is an easy-to-use but powerfully revealing tool for clearly defining what you currently want in your life.

PERSONAL STRIVINGS

When asking yourself what you want, you may feel at a loss about where to start. If you say "I want to be loved" or "I want to be famous," such broad, sweeping goals, as sincere as they are, may not lead to any clear, concrete action. On the other hand, if you say, "I want to make sure that I get the dinner cooked tonight or remember to pay the bills," you may indeed accomplish those tasks, but they may do little to change the fundamental trajectory of your life (of course, if you didn't pay the bills over several months that might indeed change your life). In defining what you want, you somehow have to find a middle path between hopelessly vague ideals and the mundane chores of daily life.

Emmons, in developing his concept of personal strivings, was acutely aware of this challenge. He wanted to find a way of measuring goals that would not be too broad or too specific. First, he realized that often psychologists and psychiatrists have been preoccupied with identifying the most fundamental drives or motives of human personality. Psychoanalysts like Freud sought to reduce all motivation to the all-encompassing drives of sex and aggression. Jung countered that our fundamental need was to find a balance between the primitive shadow aspect of our psyche and the more socially appropriate persona that served as our mask in society. Adler theorized that all human striving was reducible to our desire to overcome feelings of inferiority and realize our most positive potential. Sullivan felt that our greatest driving desire was to avoid the anxiety caused by isolation from others. Existentialists like Ernest Becker and Irving Yalom argued that we are motivated ultimately by our fear of death.

When all of our complex actions are reducible to these dominant motives, it is increasingly hard to trace back the indirect paths that would reveal their guiding force. Inevitably, theorists and therapists who make these bold claims about our desires rely on chains of inferences based on dreams, fantasies, and personality tests called projective tests (the most famous are the Rorschach and the TAT). Whether we could ever establish the ultimate truth of their claims or not (which is an issue of great debate in psychology), the average person's capacity to detect the influence of these fundamental motives in their life is likely to be quite limited. This difficulty is magnified by the fact that a number of these theorists presume that these motives and drives are out of awareness or exist in an unconscious portion of the personality to which there is no direct or easy access.

An additional problem is that even if we could boil down all your various goals or desires to an underlying drive for love or self-actualization or power, the ways that you might express this drive might differ significantly between you and the next person with the same underlying drive. For you, power might be found in being the most popular person among your friends, while for someone else a sense of power might come from getting recognition for outstanding achievements. If we are going to talk about the consistent goals that are meaningful in your life—what you most persistently hope to attain—we will need to get to a level that is much less abstract and global than these drives, needs, or motives.

Now consider again the other extreme: if we try to define your goals in the most concrete terms possible, we may indeed lose the forest for the trees. You may have the goal of getting a raise or averaging

4.0 for your GPA, but are these goals endpoints or more likely a means to some higher and more important goal? You might seek raises in order to be a better provider for your family or A's in school in order to please your parents. The practical outcomes of raises or good grades are in turn instruments to higher and more important goals.

So in between your deepest motives and your everyday goals are the middle-level goals that Emmons dubbed *personal strivings*. Personal strivings are the most important goals that you are trying to accomplish in your life—they are what you are typically trying to do. Personal strivings can be about reaching for very positive outcomes ("I typically try to be the best student in the class") or avoiding negative ones ("I typically try to avoid being the worst student in the class"). Having a personal striving does not mean you are successful in that striving or failing in it. It means simply that it is a repeated goal that you are actively pursuing.

Personal strivings can be reasonably broad ("I try to please others") or more specific ("I try to make my father proud"). They can be about "doing" ("climbing the most difficult peaks" or "keeping my belongings neat and tidy") or simply "being" ("being at peace with myself" or "being able to let go of worries"). Although individuals may share many strivings, no two individuals have exactly the same set of strivings in their lives. Clearly, your strivings can change over a lifetime, but in general your list of strivings remains fairly consistent from year to year. Major life events—beginning a career, having a child, facing a serious illness, caring for an elderly parent—will lead to realignment of your strivings and introduce new ones to the list, but a core set of concerns will always remain intact. Your list of personal strivings is your unique signature on what you are trying to accomplish in your life. It is how you write your life into the world, and consideration of these strivings provides great insight into what trajectory your current life is taking. Luckily, Emmons developed a straightforward way for you to examine your own set of personal strivings.

Creating Your Personal Strivings List

As with your memory list, it is critical that you get yourself into the best frame of mind to conduct this exercise with optimal focus and receptivity to what it can teach you. To do so, I would again suggest you give yourself some quiet time before you start. Set the book down and go for a walk, a bicycle ride, or a swim. Listen to some of your favorite music or sit down with a cup of tea. The most important thing is to let go of the pressing demands of the world for a little while and focus on yourself and your current life. If you let all the competing noises of the world remain buzzing in your brain, you will never be able to hear the elemental melodies of what is most important to you.

Now that you have done a bit of mental housecleaning, you should be ready to take on this next exercise with maximum benefit.

EXERCISE 3:
PERSONAL STRIVING INSTRUCTIONS

To start, you will need to get out your memory journal and number a clean page from 1 to 10. At the top of the page, write the phrase, "I typically try to . . . " Each of the ten personal strivings that you list will complete this sentence. Once you have your page set up, I would like you to follow these instructions modified from Emmons (1999, Appendix A). (For his research, Emmons asked for fifteen strivings, but in order to zero in on your most powerful strivings, we will focus on just ten.)

We are interested in what you typically or characteristically are trying to do. Your strivings need not always lead to success; the important point is that they express what you are repeatedly seeking to accomplish over time. For example, you might write down "try to be punctual in all situations," but in your daily life you actually fall far short of this objective. That is perfectly okay for this exercise. Your success does not matter; what is critical is that you are working actively toward that goal.

Your strivings can be about trying to attain an outcome that you desire or about trying to avoid an outcome that you do not desire. For example, you might write "I try to make my girlfriend happy" or you might write "I try to avoid making my parents angry."

Please notice that this method of describing who you are is based on actions that you take rather than adjectives to describe yourself. Do not simply list words that describe you (shy, ambitious, funny), but rather list the typical actions that characterize your most important goals.

You should make sure to write at least ten strivings and can list more if you wish. Try to focus exclusively on yourself and do not compare yourself to others. Do not dwell on what others think you should be striving for or what you think you ought to be doing. Instead, list as honestly as possible what you are really striving to do in your current life. This is your personal list and it reflects your unique set of strivings. Do not try to create a list that fits what society expects of you.

It might help to think about the major areas of your life—work or school, home and family, social relationships, and recreation/activities. In each of these areas, what might be your major goals, aspirations, and desires?

Don't rush in and write immediately. Give yourself some time to sort out what matters most and then begin to write down your list.

Once your list is done, look it over carefully and try to decide if anything is missing or if something that you wrote down doesn't truly fit. You might want to give yourself a day or two to sit with the list and see if it feels like you have got it about right. It is perfectly okay to tinker with it a bit. The process of reflecting over the list is in and of itself a valuable way of identifying what your most important priorities actually are.

Rating Your Strivings

If you feel that your list is now ready, we can proceed to the next step of working with your personal strivings. When Emmons collects strivings from individuals, he then asks them to fill out a series of 17 different ratings about the 15 strivings. That comes to 255 ratings—that's a lot of ratings! Fortunately, he has been able to boil down all these different ratings into three major ways of thinking about your strivings:

- Commitment

- Difficulty

- Desirability/reward

In other words, for each striving, you can judge how much you want it (commitment), how difficult it would be to achieve (difficulty), and how happy it would make you to reach your goal (desirability/

reward). So for our purposes, you can do three ratings per striving and these thirty ratings will give you a good sense of where these strivings fit in your life.

Exercise 4 gives you a space to write down an identifying word or phrase for each of your ten strivings on a separate row. The three columns for each row reflect your ratings from 0 to 6 for your degree of commitment, sense of difficulty, and the desirability of each goal. To make your ratings, you can pencil them directly into this table or you can record them in your memory journal.

EXERCISE 4:
PERSONAL STRIVING RATINGS

(Adapted from Emmons 1999, Appendix A)

For each of your personal strivings, please consider the three following dimensions: commitment, difficulty, and reward and rate them on the following 7-point scale:

0—Not at All

1—Slightly

2—Somewhat

3—Moderately

4—More Than Moderately

5—Very

6—Extremely

Rate your commitment to each of your ten strivings. Commitment means how important this striving is to you and how much energy you devote to it.

Next, rate the difficulty of attaining each of your ten strivings. Difficulty means how hard you think it would be to achieve this striving.

Finally, rate the desirability of each of your ten strivings. How much happiness, pleasure, satisfaction, joy, pride, and so on would you feel at attaining this striving?

Striving Name	Commitment	Difficulty	Desirability

Types of Strivings

With your striving list done and your ratings completed, we can now focus on the question of what you most want in your life and what you are doing about it. To start, let's look at the types of strivings you chose. Table 1 displays six important categories of strivings that past researchers have identified for classifying people's personal strivings.

Now in Exercise 5, you can take your ten strivings and see which categories they fit into best. Using the same identifying word or phrase from Exercise 4, list all of your strivings and then put a check mark for the category that best fits each striving. At the bottom of the table add up the total check marks that each category of striving received.

When you have finished this exercise, you should be ready to answer some of the following critical questions about your personal strivings. These questions are designed to get at key concerns about whether or not your strivings are helping to maximize positive feelings and growth in your life.

Table 1—Types of Personal Strivings

(Adapted from Emmons 1999)

- **Achievement:** accomplishing a goal; concern with success; competing; seeking excellence
    - "Put my best effort into whatever I do"
    - "Pursue future career opportunities"
    - "Achieve success in school"
- **Intimacy:** commitment to another person; warm positive interpersonal interactions; helping others
    - "Help someone I care about"
    - "Share time with someone I love"
    - "Be a good listener"
- **Power:** concern with having impact and influencing others; seeking fame and attention; competing and comparing with others
    - "Persuade others to my point of view"
    - "Be in the spotlight"
    - "Be the best in a group"
- **Personal growth and health:** improve self-esteem; improve health and fitness; increase sense of well-being and happiness
    - "Exercise daily"
    - "Feel good about myself"
    - "Be happy in life"
- **Creativity:** concern with leaving a legacy; providing for the future; creating something to last
    - "Create something new or beautiful"
    - "Contribute to my community"
    - "Be a good parent or mentor"
- **Unhealthy/self-defeating:** avoiding growth; holding self back; opposite of actions for positive health
    - "Be in a relationship no matter what"
    - "Keep my mouth shut"
    - "Be perfect at everything"

EXERCISE 5: CLASSIFYING YOUR PERSONAL STRIVINGS

Striving	Achievement	Intimacy	Power	Personal Growth and Health	Creativity	Unhealthy/ Self-Defeating
1.						
2.						
3.						
4.						
5.						
6.						
7.						
8.						
9.						
10.						
Total						

Key Questions About Your Types of Strivings

- Does one type of striving dominate all the others or is your list fairly balanced among the categories?

- Are any categories missing from your list? Does this surprise you?

- Did you have any unhealthy/self-defeating strivings? If so, how many?

- What were the total number of your strivings that fit in the categories of Achievement, Intimacy, Creativity, and Personal Health and Growth?

Research on personal strivings by Emmons, Dan McAdams, Ed de St. Aubin, and Laura King, among others, has demonstrated that people with higher numbers of intimacy and creativity strivings are likely to show a greater sense of well-being and better physical health. Similarly, a concern for personal growth and health can reflect good positive adjustment, as long as this concern doesn't dominate all other strivings. It is also valuable to have achievement strivings, but these strivings work best for you when they are balanced by intimacy and creativity strivings. In general, Patricia Linville (1985) and other social psychologists have demonstrated that when you can find your self-worth through a balance of life interests rather than exclusively in one area, you are less prone to distress and depression. This is because if something goes wrong in one part of your life, you will be able to draw on the positive aspects from other parts of your life to buffer your disappointment or frustration. When your focus is too narrowly directed, you lose the chance to switch to other parts of your life when setbacks occur.

In a similar vein, excessive emphasis on power has been linked to more anxiety, competitiveness, and at times a tendency to manipulate others for one's own ends. The presence of more than two or three unhealthy/self-defeating strivings would be a strong signal of unhappiness in your life and might serve as a red flag that the input of a counselor could be valuable.

Looking at the types of strivings you have chosen allows you to step back from your life and ask about your priorities. Are you typically doing the things that lead to your happiness and growth? Are you pursuing goals that benefit those whom you love as well as your larger community? In all honesty, does the content of your strivings reflect the person you want to be?

Having considered the types of strivings you have chosen, we are ready to consider the priority you assign them, the effort that you invest in them, and the emotion that they induce. Let's return to the ratings that you did in Exercise 4.

Commitment

Start with your Commitment ratings. Look over your ratings and look for any extremes (ratings of 0 or 1 and 5 or 6). To which of your strivings were you most committed? To which the least?

If any of your strivings received a 0 or 1, there is an important question to consider: If this striving is not important to you, then why has it made the list of the ten most important goals you are working to accomplish in your everyday life? Is this a striving you are truly seeking for yourself, or in actuality do you experience it as imposed on you by others? What do your efforts on behalf of this striving feel like for you? Is it a strain to reach this striving?

In contrast, circle any strivings that received the highest commitment scores of 5 or 6. These strivings are clearly the priority of your life and more important to you than any other competing concern. For this reason, it would be important to look at how you rate the difficulty of attaining them and also how much happiness their achievement would bring you.

Difficulty

Look over this column of ratings and try to find extremes again. Are there any strivings you perceive as easy to reach or any that you see as exceedingly difficult? Circle any of your strivings that received 5 or 6 for difficulty. We will be returning to some of these particular strivings shortly.

Desirability

Next, take note of those strivings that would bring you either the least or the most happiness once you attained them. If your goal is an activity that you try to accomplish on an ongoing basis (for example, "I typically try to treat people with respect"), then imagine the average happiness it brings to your life.

Now step back and ask yourself why you might have any strivings that would bring you little or no happiness if you achieved them. What indeed makes you pursue an outcome that brings so little positive feeling to your life? Once again, make sure to circle those strivings with the highest ratings (5 or 6) for happiness.

REACH STRIVINGS

By now you should be getting a much clearer sense of where your strivings fit in your life. You have been able to identify which types of strivings are most common in your life, and what kind of balance you are achieving among the different types of strivings. You have also tagged strivings to which you are most committed, as well as those that present the greatest challenge. You have also allowed yourself to reflect on which strivings in your life, once achieved, would bring you the greatest joy.

Since a major theme of this book is helping you to reach the goals that you are seeking, we will now zero in on those goals that present the greatest challenge to you, but would also yield the most powerful sense of happiness and satisfaction.

Let's start by going back to Exercise 4 and examining any strivings that have circles in the Commitment and Desirability columns. These strivings are very important to you and would bring great happiness to you if you were able to attain them. The fact that you are making priorities of those strivings that would bring the most pleasure to you reflects one indicator of adjustment and health.

While commitment and desirability are important, there is, however, a third factor that plays a pivotal role in how your strivings affect your ongoing life. This factor is, of course, the difficulty of getting what you want. You may have listed "find a loving partner" as your most committed striving and also the striving that is most likely to bring happiness in your life. Yet your view of how likely a prospect this striving is will fundamentally influence how hard you work for the striving, how often you ruminate about it, and ultimately your willingness to continue to list it as a striving relevant to your life.

So now check the Difficulty column for any of your strivings that already have two circles for the Commitment and Desirability columns. Start with all the strivings that are circled with extremely high scores for commitment and desirability, but are uncircled for difficulty.

What do you make of these strivings? They are strivings that you believe to be important, bring great happiness, and are no more than moderately difficult to attain. This sounds like a great combination to keep you in good spirits and functioning in a positive space in your life. We won't tinker with them, because you have found an effective formula that is working for you.

Some of you are probably thinking that this is clearly a recipe for mediocrity. If you only commit to moderately difficult goals, you might think that you will never reach any pinnacles of excellence. Aren't the most difficult challenges the sweetest goals to pursue? Just ask any Olympian or successful CEO or established artist. Weren't all their years of struggle and pursuing impossible dreams worth the ultimate prizes they achieved?

I couldn't agree more and would be sad to see lists of strivings that only contained strivings of moderate or mild difficulty. Life gains meaning from our dreams, even when we are not always able to realize them in the end. Knowing we are working toward something important, regardless of the ultimate outcome, brings great gratification to life. The problems enter when all your life is dreams and no concrete movement toward your stated objectives can be found. A striving list filled with ten impossible goals is a surefire way to foil your dreams. Individuals who perceive themselves as trying to achieve a striving but are paralyzed by the immensity of it are unlikely to make any significant progress toward success.

Ideally, our personal striving lists might have a mix of strivings that express our greatest ambitions along with a majority of strivings that keep us grounded in the realm of possibility. When high school students get ready to apply to college, their guidance counselors will tell them to draw up a list of potential schools. The list will have three parts—safety schools, good fits, and reach schools. The reach schools, the Harvards or the MITs, are long shots but would represent remarkable accomplishment and challenge due to the difficulty of attaining acceptance and the quality of the student body that attends them. The good fits are schools that suit our talents and dispositions and are likely to bring us forward in healthy and positive ways in our lives. The safety schools will also provide what we need and allow us to progress, but they may be less likely to spur us toward bursts of growth or creativity.

Turning to your own list of strivings, we have already set aside your "safety" and "good fit" strivings, so we need to place our attention on your *reach strivings*—those strivings that are high in commitment, desirability, and difficulty. Take a look at your list and find any strivings that have three circles in a row. By definition, these are reach strivings—high in importance, believed to bring happiness if attained, and perceived by you as very difficult or unlikely to come to pass.

For example, you might have a striving that fits the category of power ("I typically try to beat out the competition in any athletic challenge"). You might also rate yourself as very committed (score of 6) to this striving, that it is very difficult to achieve (6), and that it would bring great happiness (desirability) if you attained it (6). If you have any such strivings, ask yourself the following questions:

- What actions am I taking to pursue these strivings in my life?

- Is what I am doing working or not?

- Is pursuing them leading to a greater sense of happiness or meaning in my life?

- How can I know whether or not to continue to pursue these strivings?

Look carefully at these reach strivings and try to consider the role they play in your life. Do they inspire you and help you to make choices and take actions in your life? Alternatively, do you see yourself as typically trying for them more in daydreams and fantasies than in actual concrete steps toward their attainment? Are these reach strivings a helpful organizing force in your life or a source of ambivalence, regret, and potentially missed opportunities?

You might not be surprised to hear that key insights to help answer all of these questions lie in the link between your personal strivings and your self-defining memories.

LINKING YOUR SELF-DEFINING MEMORIES AND YOUR PERSONAL STRIVINGS

In the previous chapter on self-defining memories, I indicated my fascination with the enduring emotional power of memories. In trying to understand why a memory of an event from years before can maintain its ability to make us laugh or cry, I proposed a relationship between memories and the important current goals in our lives. My research studies over the years have indeed demonstrated that this relationship does exist (Moffitt and Singer 1994; Singer 1990). In my first series of experiments, I provided the participants with a list of goals and asked them to rate how important these goals were to them. I then asked them to recall a memory inspired by each goal. Once they recalled the memory, they rated it both for how strongly it made them feel and for how relevant the memory was to the success or failure of the goal that inspired it. The important result was that the more relevant a memory was to success in a desired goal, the stronger the person's positive feelings about the memory were. The opposite was also true: the more relevant the memory was to failure in a desired goal, the more negatively the person felt about the memory.

These results highlighted the close and reciprocal relationship between memories and goals. Having strongly desired goals might cause you to recall certain memories selectively—particularly those memories that support and reinforce your goals. On the other hand, it is equally possible that having a number of powerful memories about a particular goal might make you even more likely to desire or favor that goal in the future.

There was one unexpected but highly revealing finding from this first set of studies. I had been poring over the results for months when I noticed something strange about a subset of people in the study. For the most part, most participants had expressed a strong desire for certain goals and then recalled memories that supported their efforts to achieve these goals. For example, a typical participant endorsed the goal of making a success in life, recalled a memory of winning a spelling bee in school, which was relevant to the attainment of this goal, and then indicated a strong positive feeling about the memory.

There were two groups of participants who did not fit this pattern. As you might expect, individuals who were a bit more depressed tended to have more memories in which they were unsuccessful in meeting their goals. However, there was another group who showed a similar pattern of unsuccessful memories but did not show higher levels of depression. When I looked more closely at this group, I began to see that their unsuccessful memories were highly specific to certain goals and not others. At first this confused me: Why should people who were not depressed walk around with a set of memories about failing to meet their goals?

When I looked at how these people rated the goals in the list I had supplied, I started to see the answer. Most of the goals I had listed were about getting what you want (for example, achievement, love, attention, amusement, wisdom, and so on), but a small number of the goals were about avoiding what you don't want (such as failure, danger, illness). In most cases, my participants had rated the approach goals (achievement, love, amusement) very highly and given moderate or low ratings to the avoidance goals. However, there was a small but significant group of participants who showed a contrasting pattern. This group gave their strongest ratings to the avoidance goals. When I looked at the memories for this group that had been inspired by these avoidance goals, I had my answer.

Individuals who had strongly endorsed goals like avoiding failure or danger tended to have memories that were about the nonattainment of these desired goals. They recalled memories about getting hurt while getting lost at the airport or getting asthma at camp or flunking an important test. In other words, individuals who were strongly avoidant seemed to organize their memories in a different way than nonavoidant people. Most people use their memories of positive experiences as spurs to help them pursue their goals. In contrast, avoidant individuals seemed to be using their negative experiences for the same purpose—to provide evidence for why they should value their avoidance goals.

Working with my colleague Katherine Moffitt, I was able to replicate these findings with Emmons's personal striving procedure described earlier in this chapter. I found once again the same pattern—that most people recalled positive self-defining memories to support their pursuit of the goals they wanted, while avoidant individuals recalled more negative self-defining memories to serve as reminders of what they do not want to happen.

These combined results only highlighted for me the power of self-defining memories as a motivating factor in our lives. Every self-defining memory contains two critical pieces of information regarding our most important goals. First, it gives us hard data about the possibility of future success or failure in the goals we are struggling to attain. A memory about singing a successful recital in high school lets me know that I have the poise and confidence to try out for the choir in college. In a different but equally important fashion, having a memory about failing a test in college but working harder and getting an A on the final reminds me that success does not come easily and requires resilience and persistence. Coming at the same principle from the avoidant direction, a memory of a terrible time at a school dance reminds me that I prefer to socialize one-on-one.

These memories of relevant past experiences do not simply provide you with examples of likely behaviors or outcomes. The recall of the memory itself unleashes images and feelings, not just a one-dimensional printout with abstract instructions. When you recall a self-defining memory, according to the principles described in the last chapter, you are entering the memory's world during that moment of recollection, however brief, and you are reengaging your emotions with those images. You don't just recall the details of that recital and its successful outcome; you feel in the present moment the hair on the back of your neck stand up, the flush of pride throughout your body, and the triumphant smile that arcs across your face.

This emotional information supplied by your memories is just as important as any of the events of the experience. Feeling the emotion lets you know what you would be likely to feel if you attain the goal you are now seeking. It tells about the deliciousness of these feelings or, in the case of a negative outcome, the despair. If any memory of an experience from your life can serve this purpose, then self-defining memories are uniquely powerful in this regard, given their ability to invoke strong imagery and emotion. They are like your personal deck of tarot cards, a set of images with heightened symbolism ready to be recruited for anticipating and feeling the outcomes of your most desired goals.

YOUR REACH STRIVINGS AND SELF-DEFINING MEMORIES

Having stated the general relationship between memories and goals, we can turn to a specific examination of your self-defining memories and personal strivings with a special emphasis on those most challenging of strivings—your particular reach strivings.

To begin exploring this, you need to get out your list of self-defining memories. You may not have looked at them for a few days, so take a moment to read through them and reconnect with the details of each memory. Once you have done this, you might want to write out your reach strivings on a clean page in your memory journal. (If you have no reach strivings, then you might want to select the strivings that matter most to you and present at least moderate difficulty of attainment.)

Now your first step is to look for the self-defining memories that are most relevant to each of your reach strivings. Once you have done this, you are ready to answer the following questions:

- Are any of your self-defining memories relevant to the success of your reach strivings?

- Are any clearly relevant to the failure of your reach strivings?

- Did comparing your reach strivings with your self-defining memories lead to the recall of any additional self-defining memories that might be relevant to these strivings? If the answer is yes, take the time to write out this memory (or memories) and add it to your set of self-defining memories.

Continue to explore these questions until you have identified at least one relevant memory for each of your reach strivings. The memory can be either positive or negative and it can be linked to an approach reach striving or an avoidance reach striving. For example, if your reach striving is trying to avoid gossiping and saying cruel things about other people (a good example of an avoidance reach striving), then it is possible that you might have a memory of when you talked behind a friend's back.

Try to recall again the circumstances and situation in which the memory took place. Feel the emotion of shame or embarrassment that the memory can generate as you give yourself over to its imagery. Make sure that this memory does indeed have the power to stir up strong thoughts and feelings in your personality. You should repeat this process for each of the memories that you have identified as linked with your strivings. Some of these memories may be very powerful, so be sure to take your time as you move through this process and do not hesitate to get support from loved ones, friends, and/or counselors. Once you have completed thinking about and reexperiencing the memories, and confirmed their relationships and relevance to your reach strivings, you will be ready to put these self-defining memories to work for you.

MEMORIES THAT LEAD TO SUCCESS OF STRIVINGS (S.O.S.)

Are any of your self-defining memories about the success of your reach strivings? For example, if your reach striving is to be the best at your job in your department, are any of your self-defining memories about a moment of successful and outstanding accomplishment from your life, such as the time you kicked the winning goal in the regional tournament for your high school soccer team?

Whatever this success memory might be, you are going to make this memory your success of striving (S.O.S.) memory. Your S.O.S. memory is indeed your lifesaver when you feel in doubt or unsure about your abilities or potential to succeed in your reach striving. The following imagery exercise teaches you how to get the most out of your S.O.S. memory.

EXERCISE 6:
S.O.S. MEMORIES—IMAGERY EXERCISE

First, picture a concrete challenge related to your reach striving. In the earlier example, you would like to be the best in your department at work. So choose a specific step toward that goal. Perhaps it would be to move up a few places in the rankings for sales performance. Since reach strivings are very difficult, you should not start with the full realization of your ultimate goal quite yet. It is best to choose a step that would mean strong progress on your path. Once you have this step in mind, follow these steps:

1.   Choose an affirmation, such as "I know I can do this!" or "This is a goal I can reach!"

2.   You must connect your affirmation to the following statement: "I know I can do this because of what I have done in the past. In my past, I . . ." Fill in the rest of the statement with your S.O.S. memory (for example, "I kicked the winning goal in the regional tournament").

3. Now allow yourself to sit with and enter the imagery of your S.O.S. memory. To do so, follow these instructions:

    Close your eyes and take a few slow, deep breaths. Try to clear your mind of any competing or distracting thoughts. Continue to think about your statements of affirmation from steps 1 and 2. Slowly tense your toes, hold the tension for a few moments, and then let go of the tension. Repeat this holding and letting go. Then tense your upper legs for a few moments and let go. Repeat the tensing and letting go. Now tense your fists. Again, feel the tension for a few moments, then let go, and repeat. Now tense your whole arms for the same few moments and let go. Repeat this tensing and letting go in your arms. Now tense the muscles in your chest for a few moments and let go. Do this a second time with your chest. Finally, repeat two times the same tensing and letting go with the muscles in your neck and face.

    Once you have finished these relaxation exercises, you are ready to focus on your S.O.S. memory. Let the memory fully enter your consciousness. Let the positive images of your success wash over you and relive to the fullest the feelings of unabashed joy and pride at that moment. Try to see, hear, feel, and even smell again what that great moment felt like in your life. Remind yourself this is not some fantasy or idle daydream. This is a genuine memory from your own life—a moment in which all of your willpower and full ability came together to make you the best that you could possibly be. You did it before and you can do it again. Once you have this strong, good feeling reverberating inside you, you can take a few more slow deep breaths and savor the positive energy that you have created.

4. You will need to repeat step 3 over several occasions until you have solidified the link between your current efforts at your reach striving and the powerful images of your S.O.S. memory. You will know if the link is in place by noticing that your S.O.S. memory pops into your head whenever you taking a concrete step in your life toward achieving your reach striving.

Many of my clients have told me that before they practiced the S.O.S. exercises, they might have had a fleeting thought of a positive memory when working toward their most desired goals. However, after truly focusing on the S.O.S. imagery, they now rely on their self-defining memory as a powerful source of confidence and courage in facing these challenging strivings. The beauty of reliving this memory in your life is that it is a genuine testimonial to what you are capable of accomplishing—it is based on the reality of who you have been and it reminds you that you can reach those heights again.

HOW TO BE D.O.N.E. WITH NEGATIVE MEMORIES

Having emphasized that you can draw on the reality of positive self-defining memories in your life, of course we need to ask what to do about those negative memories—the memories of disappointment, of falling short or not making the grade. These memories are primary obstacles that block your positive momentum toward achieving the reach strivings in your life. If you dwell on them and let them dominate your thoughts, you will never make progress toward realizing your dreams. Yet they are also real experiences from your life and cannot be easily dismissed.

The presence of these negative memories requires a candid assessment of whether your hopes for the future have some actual possibility or not. By definition, reach strivings mean that the road ahead is difficult, so you must accept the reality of falling short at times, but you also must see the possibility of eventual success. Asking friends, relatives, coworkers, mentors, coaches, teachers, and so on, for honest feedback can help you know if continued pursuit is reasonable, but ultimately you alone must make this call.

I can recall the years that one of my brothers struggled at trying to make a success as a screenwriter in Los Angeles. Many times, my parents and I strongly questioned whether it was time for him to let go of this ambition and try to find some more reliable income. After a number of years, he finally sold a script and then went on to have a very successful career writing for film and television. There were times, I am sure, that he was the only one holding on to the firm conviction that this difficult reach striving could be attained. So there is no easy answer about when to let go or when to hold on to the strivings that matter most. Still, if you do hope to persist in pursuit of a reach striving, you will have to learn how to defuse the power of negative memories that are linked to this particular striving.

The goal of the following exercise is to assist you in this process. It teaches you how to tame some of the emotional impact of negative memories in your life and to counteract them with more positive experiences. In order to perform this exercise, you will need to look over your reach strivings and self-defining memories. Try to identify a self-defining memory that reflects a disappointment or setback with regard to one of your reach strivings. It is also possible that as you are searching through your existing set of memories, you may recall an additional memory that fits these criteria. Once you have the memory in mind, you will be ready for the Defusing of Negative Events (D.O.N.E.) imagery exercise. The goal of this exercise is indeed to help you feel that you are done returning to and brooding over the negative images and emotions associated with this memory.

EXERCISE 7: D.O.N.E. IMAGERY EXERCISE

First, picture the negative memory of disappointment and/or failure in relationship to your reach striving. For example, imagine that your reach striving is to keep a strong positive view of yourself. Your self-defining memory is of a moment as a child when you broke your sister's favorite porcelain doll during an argument and your mother called you a "wicked child." When you have this memory in mind, you must put it aside for a moment. Now look for a second self-defining memory that expresses a more successful outcome with regard to your goal. Perhaps you can recall a memory when a teacher praised your work or a time you felt particularly pleased with the way you looked before a social occasion. Once you have this memory in mind, follow these steps:

1. You will use the same relaxation technique from the S.O.S. exercise, allowing tension to build up and let go, working up your body from your toes to your head.

2. Once you are relaxed, you will need to recall the negative memory in which you failed to achieve the goal that you desire. Once you have the memory in mind, try to bring forward the images and emotions associated with

the memory. Try to notice if you are becoming more anxious and less relaxed as you think about the memory.

3. Once you notice any change in your mood or state of relaxation, you should immediately switch your thoughts to the positive memory. Concentrate on that memory until you feel yourself regaining some of your relaxed sense.

4. When you are ready, return your thoughts to your negative memory and contemplate it until you feel less relaxed again.

5. Now switch back to your positive memory until you calm down again.

6. As you gain more and more control over the negative memory, you might want to add the affirmation, "This is in the past and not who I am anymore. I am done with this memory!"

7. Repeat this process until you can think about the negative memory for long stretches without any change in the level of relaxation that you experience. It should also now be almost impossible for you to think about the negative memory without immediately invoking the images and feelings of the positive memory, as well as the healthy affirmation of your freedom from this memory's clutches.

If you work diligently at this imagery exercise, you will be able to defuse the harmful effects of negative self-defining memories in obstructing your progress toward the important reach strivings in your life. Still, it is important to acknowledge that we cannot dismiss these events from our life and pretend that they never occurred. To do so would be to live in denial of the real pain and difficulty we have faced in our life. Even more, these negative self-defining memories may have much to teach us about what we don't want, what not to do in pursuit of our goals. Yet using these memories as a source of self-knowledge and wisdom does not preclude neutralizing some of the negative emotion and second-guessing they engender. These memories can serve as catalysts for growth, not impediments to change. By defusing the negative emotion of certain memories, the D.O.N.E. exercise allows these memories to retain their value as cautionary tales to inform us rather than to linger as reminders of why we cannot succeed or reach our most desired strivings.

CONCLUDING THOUGHTS

I began this chapter by asking you what you want. By defining your most valued personal strivings, you took a step toward identifying critical goals in your life in a highly concrete manner. Even more, by labeling the themes of these strivings, you were able to look at questions of balance and healthy priorities in your life. By rating your strivings for commitment, desirability, and difficulty, you were able to determine which of your goals were currently yielding high levels of satisfaction, and which goals posed the greatest challenges. We dubbed those goals that you want the most, but simultaneously find the most difficult to obtain, reach strivings. Since we often get stuck in the pursuit of our reach strivings, I suggested some concrete ways that you could put your self-defining memories to work to encourage greater momentum toward the fulfillment of these strivings. The S.O.S. imagery exercise builds on successful self-defining memories and uses them to reinforce the positive concrete steps you are taking to fulfill your reach strivings. The D.O.N.E. imagery exercise seeks to defuse the role of negative events from your past in order to free your path to concentrate on more positive experiences.

What you want may change over the different periods of your life, but as long as you are healthy, you will always have dreams that you are working on—some prospects that lurk beyond the horizon and hold the promise of happiness or fulfillment. As you seek to answer the question of how to make these possible worlds into real ones, you will inevitably look to the past for reassurance and wisdom. Waiting there will be your self-defining memories, filled with the potent images of moments when you approached your goals and experienced success or failure. My hope is that you may learn to harness the rich potential of these memories in order to bring those strivings that dangle just out of reach into your firm and confident grasp.

3

Memories, Life Stories, and Meaning

Have you ever said, "My life is like a soap opera"? Have you ever thought, "This person's life story has more twists and turns than a good novel"? In this chapter I describe how psychologists take this comparison of our lives to works of drama and literature very seriously. In fact, a key figure in the study of personality, Dan McAdams, has declared that our identity is really no more or less than the life story that we construct over the course of our life (McAdams 1988, 1990, 1993, 2001).

We shall see how self-defining memories are vital elements of this life story that we begin to craft in early adolescence and continue to edit and revise as long as we live. We also learn about the recurring characters, plotlines, and fundamental themes that define our life stories. The stories we compose and then share of our experiences are essential to our ability to make meaning of our lives and to extract the important lessons that guide our choices and actions. To illustrate the role of stories and recurring story themes in determining our health and well-being, I provide an example of a man named Carl, who shared his story with me in psychotherapy. In learning Carl's story, we see not only ways he became trapped by its repetitive themes, but also how through therapeutic techniques he was able to extricate himself from the clutches of his confining story.

The last section of this chapter helps you to identify the components of your own life story and learn how to track recurring themes across your self-defining memories. It also provides you with concrete exercises to break free from the aspects of your story that threaten to return you over and over to negative endings. By overcoming these confines, you can find greater meaning in your life and more satisfaction in your relationships with others.

"WHO AM I?"

In the previous two chapters, you have learned how to identify important past experiences through your self-defining memories. You have also learned how to define important goals for your future. Now we turn to the question of how you weave these past and future selves into a coherent whole. What gives you an ongoing sense of sameness and unity in your life? When you look back on your life or when you look ahead, what allows you to find some common threads that connect the diverse experiences, relationships, and time periods together and prevent you from feeling fragmented and disoriented?

It used to be that the answer to "Who am I?" was easy to divine. Well into the nineteenth century, most people around the world could say: *My family lives in this village and always has. We are the sawyers or the blacksmiths or the coopers or the weavers. We are subjects of the king or the tribal leader and we go to the village place of worship to say our prayers. We will marry based on our fathers' wishes and we will raise our children to follow in our trade. Our family, community, religion, and vocation define our sense of identity.*

With the advent of the modern era, all of these certainties changed. The industrial revolution broke apart the settled lives of villagers and forced people to leave their homes to find work in cities. The promise of higher wages and easily available finished goods radically altered economies from farming to manufacturing and ultimately, in our era, to economic systems based on high technology, service, and consumerism. As mobility increased and traditional family structures broke apart, individuals also explored new religious doctrines, new attitudes about cultural values and gender roles, and often pursued choices in both work and intimate relations that broke with the expectations of their parents.

By the early twentieth century, the question "Who am I?" could no longer be simply answered by reference to one's familiar traditions and rituals. With massive migrations of people around the world and the dizzying pace of technological innovation constantly changing the nature of daily life, artistic and philosophical movements expressed themes of alienation, surrealism, and existentialism. God's very existence seemed to be in question, and for young intellectuals crises of faith and meaning abounded. In a world of chaotic upheaval, conflict, and perpetual change, individuals were forced to rely on their own devices to carve out a sense of purpose and meaning from life. Archetypal characters, like Camus's stranger who only finds meaning in his life after committing a callous murder and being condemned to death, or Humphrey Bogart's dark and haunted cinematic portrayals of private eyes or soldiers of fortune, cut off from the mainstream society, typified that century's sense of the rootlessness of "modern man."

It is no wonder that the mid-twentieth century saw the advent of the scientific study of identity. Erik Erikson (1963), the renowned psychoanalyst and founder of the field of identity research, advanced the idea that our lives are fashioned around a series of crises that define our growth or stagnation as we advance through the life cycle from birth to death. The resolution of these crises, beginning at birth with the fundamental question of trust of our caregivers and ending with a review of our life's integrity in old age, defines the particular content and shape of our unique sense of identity. Throughout all the stages of identity conflicts and crises, we attempt to perform an act of "triple bookkeeping." We seek to reconcile our bodily needs and psychological concerns with interpersonal and societal demands and influences. Each individual performs a balancing act that tilts toward one's own idiosyncratic needs, while also shifting back to acknowledge societal roles and institutions. The critical issue for Erikson and all theorists and researchers of identity is that human beings in contemporary society actively work to forge a sense of identity that gives coherence and purpose to their lives. If individuals expect to have their identities handed to them, they will often find themselves in what Erikson called a "state of diffusion" in which their lives seem to be adrift, aimless, and susceptible to despair, numbing routines, and social isolation.

Beginning in the 1980s, McAdams (1988, 1990, 1993, 2001) proposed a highly original way of thinking about Erikson's depiction of the struggle to forge a sense of identity. Drawing on advances in the social sciences and humanities in the study of narrative, McAdams argued that the fundamental way that contemporary individuals in Western societies locate a sense of identity is through the crafting of a life story. In our efforts to define ourselves and determine where we belong in the world, we reach out to the stories we have learned from our culture's myths, fairy tales, songs, literature, film, television, advertising, and all other media that contain characters, plots, and themes from which we might draw. Weaving together these diverse influences, we fashion a story of our lives, beginning in early adolescence (when we first have the intellectual capacity to step back and reflect more abstractly on our lives) and evolving over all the decades of our adult years until we reach life's end.

Perhaps the most radical assertion of McAdams's life story theory of identity is that the life story is not a story about identity, but is identity itself. The story that you create over the course of your life is the most powerful way that you come to know yourself, as well as the most meaningful way in which others come to know you. In other words, if I want to know who I am, I need to know my story. If I want you to know who I am, I need to tell you my story. And if you want me to know you, you need to tell me yours.

In this view of personality and identity, every person in the society is both an author and a protagonist of a unique and lifelong saga. McAdams's life story theory is a perfect fit for a culture that values the integrity and complexity of each individual life. In a media-saturated society, it gives prominence to the act of storytelling and in a sense allows each of us to be a star of an ongoing and evolving tale. In the course of telling our story, we are able to identify the important characters that play prominent roles; we are able to describe familiar settings to which we often return; we can highlight prominent turning points and setbacks; and we can ultimately determine the major themes that help to explain the overall meaning of the story.

Through all these storytelling devices, we create a sense of continuity, purpose, and belonging, which is so difficult to achieve in contemporary society. A good story—the sense that we have organized and lived our life to a positive end—allows us to experience some contentment and peace in an otherwise turbulent world. In contrast, individuals who cannot link the jagged edges of their lives together into a coherent narrative, who experience their worlds as disjointed, contradictory, or lacking any forward movement, often wrestle with confusion and despair.

THE TOOLS OF THE LIFE STORY

How do you craft your story? What are the raw materials and tools in your life that you use to make an identity story that fits for you? McAdams has described the following key ingredients: setting, themes, characters, key episodes, structure, and endings. Let us review each of these components of the life story, adding the element of meaning-making, and then see how they all work together in the identity story of one of my clients from my therapy practice.

Setting

Your life story setting is not so much a physical setting, but more a state of mind that you repeatedly bring to your story. By adolescence, your childhood experiences have given you an overall sense of how things go in the world. If life has gone relatively smoothly up to that point and you have felt supported in your development, you are likely to see the world in optimistic terms. People are generally good; things usually work out; no problem is insurmountable. On the other hand, if you have already seen your share of disappointment, cruelty, and failure, you may see tragedy or rejection lurking around every corner. You may be slow to trust people and to let them trust you. Where others see hope, you may see one more instance of injustice.

Your setting, then, is the general worldview that you bring to your story. Its palette—bright or dark—gives the overall hue to the events and people that fill in your story.

Theme

McAdams, along with many other contemporary psychologists, has suggested that contemporary Western society is dominated by the search for balance between two overriding concerns—the need for individuality and freedom (agency) and the need for connection and closeness (communion). As you struggle to define yourself in this society, you constantly feel the pull between these two motives—what Freud once defined as "love and work." Each of us forges our own relative balance between these two overarching motivations. Those individuals who are higher in communion are likely to organize their lives around relationships. They put family and friends first. They would not work late at the expense of a friend's baby shower or skip their daughter's school play in order to have dinner with a prospective business client.

Others, who put agency first, might delay marriage in order to establish a successful career. Individuals with higher levels of agency might reject a place in the family business in order to forge an independent success of their own. They might find as much satisfaction in solving a thorny problem from work as they would in sharing an intimate conversation with a friend.

Individuals high in both agency and communion constantly juggle priorities in their lives in order to meet both achievement and intimacy goals. When the balancing act works, they may feel like they have it all; when it teeters near collapse, they may feel overstressed and frustratingly empty.

Each person's life story returns to these two dominant themes. As we accumulate our life's unfolding chapters, the pages within these chapters reflect the degree to which pivotal life moments and decisions express our need to define ourselves separate from or linked to others. Did you take your first job out of college to live closer to your girlfriend or to break away from an unhealthy relationship? Did you push your son to stand on his own two feet or did you emphasize his obligations to family and tradition? Did you choose to reenlist in the service to pursue promotion, even though it would mean more time away from family? Did you decide not to work after the birth of your first child?

> **Your life story is a story of separation and connection. These themes pervade its narrative and provide it with an ongoing dynamic tension.**

Characters

All good stories are built on the interactions of characters, and your life story is no exception. In most episodes from your life story you are the main character, but this is not absolutely necessary. In a simultaneously comic and sorrowful short story by Delmore Schwartz (1978), "In Dreams Begin Responsibilities," a man finds himself in a movie theater, watching a film of his parents' courtship years before his birth. Knowing the unhappiness into which their eventual marriage would devolve, he screams out in the darkened theater and tells them to stop, that no good will come of this union. Ultimately, he wakes from this dream, facing his actual life on a cold winter morning.

We can indeed incorporate into our life stories important episodes from others' lives or historical events that we have not ourselves witnessed, but in general we are direct participants in the stories that we craft, and we are also the central protagonists. However, we fill the stories we tell with other significant figures—heroes, villains, wise counsels, and naive child figures, trusted confidantes, and shadowy betrayers. Among the countless cast of characters across all the many episodes of our lives, we do indeed blend individuals into archetypal characters, what McAdams, borrowing from Jung, calls *imagoes.*

These imagoes or archetypes are the recurring types that play critical roles at different junctures in our lives. In each of our personal stories, we select a different set of these prominent archetypal individuals. Fitting with the overarching themes of agency and communion, these characters usually represent some blend of these two motives.

For example, one of my clients constantly returned to the character of a beautiful and vulnerable woman who combined both a depth of heart and an unquenchable sadness. He first fell for a girl in high school who personified this haunted beauty character. He found another woman with these qualities in college, and this was how he characterized the woman with whom he was currently having an affair. My client's life story had come to highlight his search for a woman who held the unfulfilled promise of a perfect form of romantic and spiritual communion. The setting of his life has taught him that this pursuit led to eventual heartbreak and loss, but he could not resist the allure of these characters.

From this description, it should be clear that McAdams means more than the idea that any life story will have a cast of characters in it. He means more precisely that we populate our life stories with characters that come to symbolize something beyond themselves. These archetypal characters reflect our stories' particular emphasis on the relative value and power of autonomy and connection in our lives.

Key Episodes

Every story is made up of events, actions, reactions, and outcomes. Your life story consists of key events or episodes that are particular turning points or touchstones in your larger narrative. If you think of your life story as having certain chapters that encompass periods of your life (for example, high school, college years, early years of marriage, first years of parenthood, and so on), then in each period there are likely to be key episodes (what McAdams calls *nuclear episodes*) that stand out and help to clarify important themes from that period.

These key episodes, which are really a subset of self-defining memories, might consist of a triumph or defeat in your life, a moment when an important relationship began or ended, or an instance when you became aware of something you had never understood before about yourself, someone else, or the world. These key episodes include what psychologists call *peak experiences*, moments of intense vitality, joy, and sudden insight, or *nadir experiences*, where life hits bottom and is filled with overwhelming pain or despair. Key episodes in the life story are those self-defining memories that stand out as the most important and pivotal among all possible memories of your life.

William Todd Schultz (2002) has referred to these key episodes as *prototypical scenes* from your life story and suggested that these scenes often contain the blueprints of your life concerns and themes within them. We can trace this idea of key episodes or prototypical scenes as crucial components of the life story directly back to Silvan Tomkins's script theory, as described in chapter 1 of this book. These key episodes contain plots, strong emotions, and outcomes that are likely to be repeated as familiar patterns in our lives.

For example, McAdams has spent a great deal of time in recent years studying the pattern of redemption and contamination in the life stories of individuals. Redemptive scenes are key episodes in which something that starts out bad leads ultimately to a more positive outcome (redemption). An individual might recall memories of how a painful divorce taught her to be more independent and trust her own abilities and opinions in life. Similarly, a person may recall how a firing from a job led her to start her own company that has become highly successful. A third person might recall how the death of a close friend taught him to devote his life to helping others.

In contrast to these redemption scenes, other individuals might be prone to recall key episodes of their life that go in the opposite direction—from good to bad (contamination). For example, a successful doctor recalls how his thriving practice was nearly destroyed by a malpractice suit. A middle-aged woman recalls how her childhood dinners would start with hope and end with her father's bitter arguments with her mother. A student of great promise recalls repeated examples of beginning, but not finishing, ambitious creative works.

By studying these repetitions of themes, plots, characters, and sequences of emotions across a series of key episodes in our lives, we can learn about the critical concerns and, sometimes, the self-defeating patterns that define our life stories of identity. In the exercise portion of this chapter, I help you to look for these patterns in your own self-defining memories. Once identified, we can then consider how you might escape from their grasp.

Structure

Every story has a structure. It can be straightforward and easy to follow with a simple linear plotline and few twists and turns. In the simplest life story structure, you grow up in the same house, graduate from the local high school, go the local college, get married after graduation, buy a home close to your parents, take a job with the town's biggest employer, have two children, stay married to the same person your whole life, retire at sixty-five, spend time with your grandchildren, and depart this world in a peaceful sleep at age ninety, only to be buried in the family plot a mile from the home in which you were born. Of course, most of us no longer (if we ever did) have narratives that form such a clear and uninterrupted straight line. Our stories veer into tangents, double back and plunge forward, get waylaid in repetitive loops, and finally stagger toward some kind of finish line.

How we tell our stories—the amount of nuance, complexity, and ambiguity we introduce—has a lot to say about how we think about our lives. Individuals with rather direct and unembellished life narratives tend to be more practical and concrete thinkers. They shade toward conventional values and viewpoints in how they assess the world. Individuals who give their stories more ornate and convoluted structures tend to be a bit more tolerant of multiple perspectives in their worldviews and a little bit more patient with life circumstances that lack any easy answers.

In addition to the overall life story structure, we may also consider the structure of the individual self-defining memories and key episodes. In my many years of studying self-defining memories, I have detected two important structural types of self-defining memories—*specific memories* and *summary memories*. Specific memories are tied to specific moments in time and employ distinct and pointed imagery to convey that moment. Here is an example of a specific memory from one of my research participants:

I can remember the day my church group made it to the top of Mount Washington. The wind was blowing so hard that we had to hold hands to keep from blowing off the side of the mountain. Our faces were frozen and I could see little icicles on the beard of our group leader. We were freezing, but the sense of pride and community we had made all our physical discomfort seem trivial. We looked out over all the white hills below and gave praise to the Lord.

This memory can be traced to an exact day and time when the events took place. Its imagery brings us back to the specific events of the memory and makes it easy to reexperience the particular emotions of awe, pain, and exhilaration that the narrator felt.

Now in contrast, consider the following summary memory, also from one of my research participants:

When I was growing up my mother could never find a good word to say to me. No matter what I did she was sure to find a flaw. We would have these moments where she would make her critical comment and then seem to wait for a reply. I remember so many times holding my tongue, going off to my room, and just burying my head in my pillow.

Although this memory is about an important theme from the person's life—her mother's repeated criticism—we cannot trace the memory to any one particular example or instance of their negative interactions. If we want to reexperience what it felt like for this person to interact with her mother, we would have to conjure up our own imagery and create an imagined specific scene in which her mother behaved critically. The summary quality of the memory keeps us and, we can assume, the narrator one step removed from the actual images and emotions associated with the specific events described in the memory. This distance may help to protect this person from having to reexperience the specific painful emotions implied, but not portrayed, by the memory.

Our research has indeed demonstrated that individuals who score higher on a measure of defensiveness show a greater number of these summary memories and fewer specific memories. These defensive individuals who are inclined to deny the presence of negative emotion in their lives have apparently adopted a strategy of remembering that provides them with some distance from the powerful imagery and emotion that self-defining memories can invoke.

Interestingly, our studies found that these individuals were likely to recall similar numbers of negative memories as individuals who were less defensive. However, the key difference was that more defensive individuals kept their memories (positive and negative) at greater arm's length with regard to specificity and imagery. It is as if they were willing to look, but only so far. As long as they could keep their memories in this summary state, they were willing to acknowledge both highs and very deep lows in their lives. Yet acknowledging them intellectually is different from allowing the emotion of the memories to reenter their lives.

Structure then can come in two forms—the complexity of the overall story and the specific nature of a given memory. Both of these structural aspects of the life story can provide insight into your flexibility and willingness to engage with the more complicated themes and powerful emotions of your life.

Endings

As we move through our lives compiling the unified story of the different periods of our lives, we are always looking toward the future and asking ourselves the questions, "How will it turn out in the end?" "What will my legacy be?" In Mark Twain's *The Adventures of Tom Sawyer*, Tom and Huck are presumed dead and they have the inestimable opportunity to sneak into the rafters and observe their own funeral. This is a wish that all of us entertain—to know how others will think of our life and to have the peace of mind that we will be remembered with both love and respect by family, friends, and perhaps even the larger community. Erikson referred to this concern for our legacy and our impact on future generations as *generativity*, and it forms one of his eight psychosocial stages of the life span. Its opposing force is *stagnation*, the sense that you have not allowed yourself to act on your creative processes and that your life feels barren of contribution and promise.

In McAdams's life story theory, how we see our story ending—whether with a sense of a productive life embedded in relationships or in a hollow demise, isolated and thwarted in ambition—reflects the final critical component of our life narrative. The other components—our overall tone of hope or dread, our respective emphasis on autonomy or connection, our recurring characters, and our key episodes—all converge on the question of how much our story has mattered in the end and to whom. We seek a legacy for reasons related to agency: to acknowledge that we were here, that we lived, worked, and made our unique presence in the world known. We also seek it for communal reasons: to secure a world beyond our lives for the people whom we have loved, to make sure they are able to go forward once we are gone and that their lives are built on a positive and solid foundation.

Here then is a remarkable way of thinking about what your identity is and who you really are. You hold the answer to where you fit in this world—what your place is in your family life, your circle of friends, and the wider society. The answer lies in the story of your life that you yourself are authoring. Combining your setting, themes, characters, key episodes, and endings, you continually add to and revise this self-defining narrative that lets you know what matters most to you and, through its telling, informs others as well. In recent years, many other psychologists besides McAdams have come to see that this life story and its self-defining memories are sources of meaning-making and wisdom for individuals as they move through their adult lives. Let us then add one final component to the life story—the role of meaning-making.

Meaning-Making

It is not enough to tell your story. You need to make sense of the stories you tell. If you are able to step back from your stories and look at their implications for your life, you can then make full use of the powerful structures of identity that you have forged. In a special issue of the *Journal of Personality* (June 2004), I assembled a series of articles by prominent researchers that illustrated exactly this theme. Individuals who could step back from the key memories of their lives and extract a moral or lesson from these experiences showed better adjustment, higher levels of maturity, and more wisdom compared to other individuals with less capacity for meaning-making. These findings were true for both positive and negative experiences, but particularly for difficult experiences. As the work of James Pennebaker (1995) has also demonstrated, our ability to see a purpose or an ultimate meaning in even the most traumatic experiences in our lives is associated with greater psychological and physical health.

In my work on self-defining memories, my colleague Pavel Blagov and I demonstrated that the more meaning-making statements individuals included in their written descriptions of self-defining memories, the healthier outlook and better coping strategies they showed in their lives overall (Blagov and Singer 2004). Meaning-making statements included phrases like "This experience taught me that . . ." "Ever since that event, I have realized that . . ." "This memory was a turning point for me because . . ." Statements like these indicate that you have stepped back from this key event and attempted to see where it fits in the larger picture of your life. You have not just had the experience, but you have put it to work for you as a form of self-knowledge and growth.

With this last component in place, we are ready to look at the role of the life story and meaning-making for Carl, an angry but ultimately well-intentioned man who came to see me in my therapy practice.

CARL'S STORY

Carl, a forty-year-old man of Mexican-American descent, was born in Texas, but moved to Arizona as small boy with his mother. His father had walked out on the family when Carl was still an infant and his mother had no further contact with him. Carl's mom remarried when he was still a toddler, and so he grew up with her and his stepfather as parents. Carl's stepfather made it clear to Carl early on that he was not his son, and often treated him quite cruelly and violently. Though Carl asked his mother about his biological father, she refused to give him any information about his father.

The family lived in poverty, and Carl grew up learning to be tough in a rough neighborhood. Perhaps from fights on the block, he learned how to wrestle and eventually became an outstanding wrestler at the regional and state level. Part of his drive for wrestling was the fact that he was very small and often felt that people expected him to be weak or a pushover. He certainly overcompensated for his short stature; he was made of pure muscle and, pound for pound, was one of the strongest and most intimidating individuals you might ever meet.

Another factor that contributed to his success as a wrestler, but his struggles elsewhere, was his deep reservoir of rage. Although able to channel it into fierce competition on the wrestling mat, he sometimes let his temper flare in the rest of his life. At such moments, and they were usually moments when his sense of adequacy felt threatened, he seemed primed to pounce like a cornered panther. He could lash out with vicious words, start physical fights, and damage property. These behaviors had led to some arrests for disturbing the peace and disorderly conduct over the last twenty-five years. However, he had gained control over these behaviors substantially in the last few years and limited himself to only verbal displays of his anger.

Carl received an athletic scholarship to a state university and graduated with a degree in criminal justice. This degree was a bit ironic in that he had developed a lucrative "numbers" business on the side during his college years. Carl's illegal gambling business became an important dimension of his life for the next ten years. With his forceful (not to mention intimidating) personality and quickness with figures, Carl found that he could take in an income of nearly $1,000 a week from this side business.

Soon after college, he met his wife, who was a nursing student at the university, and after six months of dating, they married. He took on a legitimate job of selling office information systems, but kept up the bookie business, even after multiple promises to his wife to stop. They had one child, a son, who was a very successful student and athlete, though also very strong willed and short-tempered like his father.

Over the nearly fifteen years of their marriage, Carl and his wife grew increasingly distant. He kept the world of his gambling racket secret from her and she focused more and more on her advancement in the nursing profession. Eventually, their estrangement and quarrels reached a level where his wife asked him for a divorce. Carl was devastated by this rejection, even though he could not say that he felt in love with his wife any longer. One positive outcome of their failed efforts to preserve their marriage was that Carl had quit the gambling business and finally left these activities behind him for good.

Within a year of his divorce, Carl took up with Sandy, a very attractive, educated professional woman, who was in her thirties and never married. Sandy, a highly emotional person who was inclined to abuse alcohol, had a history of volatile relationships that would move toward marriage, but then crash and burn in bitter ways. After an initial courtship that moved rather gradually, Carl found himself passionately in love with Sandy, but also in frequent and explosive conflicts with her. At the same time, he was increasingly arguing with his son, who was preparing to go to college. As if these two conflicts were not enough, Carl also had become at odds with a very domineering and manipulative boss at work. Feeling embattled from all directions, Carl came to see me in order to work on his problems with anger and the relationships in his life.

Making Sense of Carl's Story

After a few meetings with Carl, it was not hard to see how difficulties with other people surfaced in his life. He would call me on a day that we were not scheduled to meet and suggest that it might be more convenient for him to come that day than at our scheduled meeting time. When I would decline to switch our time, given that he was not in a crisis, he would express his displeasure in a rather gruff fashion. When we reached a point of discomfort in a meeting, he would sometimes narrow his eyes and stare at me in an intimidating fashion. I continued to call his bluff on these behaviors and he very soon acknowledged that this was his usual pattern—to try to take control in situations before the other person did. Luckily, he had a good sense of humor about his default "bully" behavior and we were soon able to put aside that dynamic in our work together.

As Carl settled into his relationship with me and became more trusting, we went to work on understanding the life story that defined his identity and self-understanding. Carl's settings tended to depict the world as filled with suspicion and betrayal. He expected others, whether father, stepfather, ex-wife, new girlfriend, or boss, to turn on him and reject him.

Carl's themes of agency and communion revealed a fascinating tension. On one hand, he had always fought to define himself as a powerful and independent individual. Yet he recognized that his bravado often hid his deep sense of inadequacy, a conviction that he could only be successful through manipulation, "sleazy behavior," and intimidation of others. In contrast, he had always been someone who felt a deep yearning for connection despite his outward toughness. He could come to tears in talking about his love for his son or his painful quarrels with his girlfriend. Now in middle age, he knew that more than any monetary success or business success, he wanted to feel that he had achieved a stable, loving family life. So despite an outwardly independent demeanor, it would be fair to say that Carl's most powerful goals were much more relationship oriented than individualistic.

Carl's major life story characters said much about his difficulty with trusting others. One recurring character we immediately see is the angry father character. With a biological father who left him as an infant, an alcoholic and abusive stepfather, or a domineering boss, Carl inhabited his life story with male authority figures who hurt him and provoked him.

Another recurring character is the woman casting judgment. Dating all the way back to his mother, Carl felt the women in his life saw him as "someone less than" and a "negative force" in their lives. He felt at some level that his mother blamed him for his father leaving her, perhaps due to the responsibility that having a child posed to him. Carl also felt that his presence caused tension and problems between his mother and stepfather, and that she resented him for his role in these arguments.

Later, during his marriage, he knew that his wife condemned him for his gambling business. As she moved forward in her nursing career, he felt less and less respect from her and increasingly the focus of her disapproval and judgment. Now in his current relationship with a highly educated and professional woman, he often felt like a "back-woods bum from the wrong side of the tracks" or a guy with a "sleazy past."

In his relationship with his son, Carl sought desperately to avoid being the angry father figure that haunted his own life. However, at moments of conflict, he could see himself moving into this role and becoming highly intimidating toward his son. Whether interacting with his son, attempting to deal with his boss at work, or working through an argument with his girlfriend, Carl felt the constant presence of these archetypal characters in his life and sometimes found these roles, rather than his own free will, seemed to dominate his emotions and behaviors.

Carl could recall several key episodes that expressed the central themes of his life story. He described one self-defining memory in which his stepfather told him that he was glad that Carl was not his real son and that he wished Carl's father had taken Carl with him the day that he left his mother. When we discussed the meaning of this memory for Carl, he was able to say with great emotion that he wondered if he could ever be good enough for someone to really want him or if he was just "damaged goods."

Another memory that was pivotal for Carl was when his son opened a drawer in a desk at home filled with betting slips. He felt immense shame at this illegal past and his son's discovery of it. Carl connected this memory to a more recent memory when his girlfriend found that he had retained a list of phone numbers of women that he had dated prior to meeting her. He knew this discovery revealed the manipulative distrustful side of him that was always looking for another angle or fallback plan.

These key episodes captured powerfully Carl's pattern of feeling "less than" and how he connected his deceptive "outlaw" activities to these feelings. These memories revealed the strong sense of shame he experienced when he attempted to patch over his feelings of inadequacy with either manipulation or intimidation. Additionally, he also expressed a sense of relief and freedom when he came clean and let go of these secretive or negative activities. From these memories, then, we can identify a critical script for Carl:

Feeling inadequate

↓

Deceptive or threatening behavior

↓

Confrontation

↓

Shame

↓

Confession

↓

Relief

Carl desperately wanted to see his story end in a more positive fashion. He wanted to improve his relationship with his son and to resolve his stormy relationship with his girlfriend. He also sought to see himself in a positive fashion and to feel that he could live his life in a more honest and less manipulative fashion.

Finally, Carl's capacity for *meaning-making*, or what therapists call "insight," is critical to his therapeutic goals. If Carl were to change, he would need to learn how to step back from his story's pages and read between the lines. He must learn how to interpret and make sense of his emotional reactions and subsequent behaviors. The more that he could see how the script outlined above sends him into repeated negative behaviors, the more likely he would be to exert the self-control to stop this self-defeating pattern.

HELPING CARL TO CHANGE

Over the months of therapy with Carl, we were able to define his life story and the key components described earlier. Carl could see how this story would often influence his responses to his son, girlfriend, or boss. He could further see how when he let it play out without stepping back, the same old negative conflicts and episodes of anger and shame would occur. Now to break the cycle, we first made sure Carl could identify the scripted sequence and could locate examples of it in his current interactions. We then began to develop strategies to change this pattern. There are three critical interventions to highlight:

- Defining true wants

- Role-playing

- Breaking the cycle

Defining True Wants

This technique goes directly back to William Glasser's reality therapy approach that I described in the previous chapter. Working with Carl, we clarified his overarching goals for this period of his life. He stated emphatically that he wanted to control his anger and forge better relationships in his life. He also stated without equivocation that he wanted to live an honest and authentic life. He resonated very strongly with my description of the pillow test (described in chapter 2) and set as a primary goal the ability to go to bed each night feeling that he had not been deceptive and coercive in his interactions with others.

These goals—to achieve more trusting relationships and live a more authentic life—were the clear answers to "What I do want?" Knowing these answers, he could then apply this simple mantra to any challenging interpersonal interaction and ask the follow-up question, "Is what I am doing or about to do bringing me closer to or further from my goals?"

Carl found this breakdown of complicated interpersonal interactions into these basic questions very helpful. Combined with some relaxation techniques (taking slow breaths and drawing on comforting images), he was increasingly able to slow down his familiar angry and impulsive reactions to situations in which he felt threatened. He saw that the real goal in such situations was not to protect his momentarily bruised ego or to put the other person down, but ultimately to do what would be best for improving his relationship with that person, while at the same time maintaining a positive view of his own honesty and integrity.

Carl also found it particularly helpful to use memories of interactions in the past where things had gone awry to warn him not to fall into the same old trap. He could simply say to himself, "Not another telephone list moment," and it would remind him that to deceive his girlfriend or go behind her back would only deepen the divide between them.

Role-Playing

To solidify this learning, we often engaged in role-playing exercises in therapy. I would play Carl's boss and make a comment that would put Carl on the defensive. Carl would practice stepping back from the situation and first doing some "self-talk." For example, he would say to himself, "My boss is not my stepfather. Even if he is wrong in what he says, I can't let my anger from years ago get in the way here." Next, he would ask himself what he wanted in the situation. Since his goal was to avoid an escalation of conflict at work, he would choose a course of action that would support this goal. He would speak his response out to me, and I would continue to play out a set of responses from his boss. Through several repetitions of these types of exercises over the weeks, Carl became much more skilled in keeping a positive focus during situations when he might previously have exploded or lost his cool.

Breaking the Cycle

Sometimes, just thinking through the situation or role-playing was not enough for Carl. In these cases, we agreed that it might be helpful to have his girlfriend or son come into the therapy office and talk out some of their difficulties. Although with many clients these opportunities might not be possible, when the family members or significant others are agreeable, this can be one of the most powerful interventions of all.

With the other person there, I was able to help Carl directly check out some of the negative assumptions that he brought to interactions with people that he loved. In this way we could challenge both the settings and the character roles that his scripts imposed on other people. When he could hear in a safe and nonconfrontational environment that some of his imposed ideas were just the vestiges of his memory scripts, it went a long way to helping him gain the trust that he needed to let go of some of his suspicions and fears. These direct experiences were powerful antidotes to his scripts and helped to break the self-defeating cycle they created for him.

Carl continued to have his moments of struggle in his close relationships, but he also saw vast improvement in them, not to mention a tremendous growth in comfort with himself. He found indeed that most nights he could pass the pillow test with flying colors and that the endings he imagined to his life story held more hope and happiness than ever before.

YOUR LIFE STORY

In order to uncover your life story and identify its themes, characters, key episodes, and endings, we will draw on recommendations from McAdams (1993), as well as some of the methods that I have used with my clients over the years. To conjure up your own life story it is helpful to collect aids from your past that will bring back memories, people, and important events.

Table 2 lists a variety of ways that you might enlist memory aids. Although it might be difficult to track down many of these materials, the goal is to give you an idea of the full range of memory devices that can assist your life story review. Many of my clients have engaged in very thorough and productive life story reviews without any of these aids, and some have employed almost all of them. There is no right way to go about creating your life story review, but it is helpful to know that these aids might be available and serve as effective spurs to important memories from the different periods of your life.

Table 2: Memory Aids for Your Life Story Review

1. Photo albums (if possible, see if you can borrow albums from your parents or grandparents as well)

2. Yearbooks from primary school, middle school, high school, and college

3. Prizes, trophies, favorite souvenirs, and mementos from different periods of your life

4. Collections of letters (letters written during summer camp periods, time abroad, college years, and over the course of relationships are often very revealing)

5. Journals or diaries that you have kept (some people are diligent enough to have kept continuous diaries over their entire lives)

6. Copies of admission essays (for example, college admission essays, graduate or medical school personal statements, fellowship applications, and so on)

7. Autobiographical writing that you might have done for school assignments or purely for your own interest

8. Videotapes from key events in your life (such as confirmation, wedding, bar or bat mitzvah, high school or college graduation, school play, concert recital)

9. Personal Web sites or blogs that you have set up over the years that may convey insight into your interests, priorities, and more passionate pursuits

10. Materials that convey how others have viewed you (letters of recommendation, report cards with teachers' evaluations, summer camp counselors' letters about you to your parents, testing results, supervisors' evaluations of job performance, and so on)

As you assemble these memory aids, do not hesitate to ask family members, friends, and colleagues for help, input, or feedback.

It may take some time to accumulate these materials and many of them may no longer be available to you, but if you can take the time, it is well worth the process of digging out as much of this information as possible. I am hoping that you see this effort to review your life story as a unique opportunity to step back and examine in the most fundamental terms who you have been, how you have fared in life, and how you have been received by others.

Most of the time we barely catch our breath and then race on to the next accomplishment, commitment, challenge. This exercise asks you to slow down, gather up the traces you have left in your path, and look back. In this break from your life's inhalations and exhalations, you can see more clearly what has been most important to you and how the world has responded to the goals you have set for yourself. My hope is that you will also see how some turns in your life have launched you forward and how others have led to dead ends. The ultimate goal of this exercise is for you to gain greater ownership of and control over your life story by making it more explicit and apparent to your conscious mind.

As you gather materials together (and it may take several days, depending on how thorough you choose to be), you should also make sure to review your self-defining memories and keep them close at hand. With your memory aids and your set of self-defining memories in place, you are ready to tell your story as comprehensively and openly as possible. There are a number of ways that you can approach the telling of your life story.

EXERCISE 8: REVIEWING YOUR LIFE STORY

- Try to write your life story out in a memoir fashion, but don't worry about the elegance or perfection of your prose. Just get the critical events down and keep your momentum going so that you don't bog down. The goal is not to write your autobiography quite yet, but instead to get the big events and themes covered in a chronological fashion.

- Turn on a tape recorder and speak your story out loud. This may help you get the job done faster, especially if you are prone to writer's block. The problem is that it is a little hard to go back later and track down specific sections for more careful scrutiny.

■ Create an illustrated storybook—a kind of scrapbook with more extended explanations of the pictures and objects that you have pasted inside. It can be divided by periods of your life (for example, infancy, childhood, teen years, early adult years, and so on) or even year by year. It depends on how successful you've been in finding memory aids and how good your memory for specific events of your life might be.

■ If you are more of a visual thinker and not inclined to use words to express yourself, you could also select the important periods from your life and attempt to create a visual representation of key moments from that period. You could do this in any medium (such as pencil, ink, watercolor, oil, or collage) in either a more representational or abstract fashion. The key to working in this fashion is to ask yourself both what this visual depiction means to you and how it makes you feel when you view it.

Once you have some version of your life story set down in prose, tape, or picture (or some combination of all three), you are ready to answer a series of questions about your unique life story.

EXERCISE 9: TRACKING YOUR LIFE STORY

(Adapted from McAdams 1993)

1. Imagine the life story that you have depicted as a good thick novel. What would be the chapter titles that you might give to the major periods of your life? In your memory journal, write out a "table of contents" for your life and put each chapter title on a line.

2. Within each period that you have designated as chapter, try to identify and give titles to the key episodes from this chapter. Are there any turning point memories that you can locate in this period? Are there any peak experiences of intense joy or nadir experiences of extreme

despair? How many of these key episodes were already identified as your self-defining memories?

3. Taking each chapter separately, try to make a list of the most important people from this period of your life. For each person, make a brief list of the words or phrases that capture this person's most typical characteristics. Pay special attention to those characteristics that reflect either the more agentic (individualistic) or communal (relational) qualities of their personalities. Look especially to see if certain character types repeat across the chapters of your story.

4. Once you have listed your chapter headings, your key episodes, and your most important characters, step back from the life story that you have identified. Now think about the story as a whole and imagine that you have to summarize its overall moral or lesson to a friend. What might be the brief sentence or two that you would use to describe your story's overarching theme to this person?

Once you have finished laying out the various components of your life story, you are ready to look for the key themes and patterns that help you to understand your own unique identity. Here are some next steps that you can take toward greater insight into the meaning of your life story.

EXERCISE 10: FINDING PATTERNS IN YOUR LIFE STORY

1. **Life story chapters:** Look over the chapter titles you have chosen. Do you divide your life up more by agentic or communal themes? Are you more an "achievement" or a "relationship" person? How do your chapter titles correspond to the list of goals that you created in the previous chapter? What is the balance in your chapters between agency and communion?

2. **Memory patterns:** Take all of your self-defining memories and key episode memories (there may be substantial
overlap among these memories) and read them through
very carefully. What repetitions or patterns do you see?
In order to find patterns it may help to do the following
exercise:

   a. Try to identify the sequence of emotions in each
   memory. Does the memory start with a happy scene,
   go to a disappointment, and end with a return to
   positive feelings? Does it begin with sadness, move to
   anger, and end in guilt or shame? There are countless
   patterns that feelings can follow, but your goal is to
   see if you can spot the patterns that repeat.

   b. Once you have mapped out the emotion sequences
   and looked for repeated sequences, try to decide if
   your memories reveal a redemption or contamination script. To remind you, redemption memories go
   from negative to positive and contamination
   memories go from positive to negative.

3. **Character patterns:** Take all the character descriptions
from your various chapters and look them over very
carefully to see the mix of agentic and communal
characteristics that they convey. Who are the heavily
agentic characters in your life story? Who are the heavily
communal ones? How do these depictions correspond to
expected gender roles? Are there any unusually agentic
women? Are there any heavily communal men?

   What types of characters seem to occupy the
villain roles for you in your life? What do they have in
common with each other? Who occupies your hero
roles? Do you see any mentorlike figures? What characters seem to hurt you the most? What characters soothe
you and come to your rescue? What characters provoke
the most envy in you? What characters serve as your
confidantes?

4. **Structure patterns:** Consider carefully the flow of your
life story. Is it direct or circuitous, filled with linear
sequences or twisted like a pretzel with ups and downs

and sideways digressions?

Next look at your key episodes (including all of your self-defining memories) and consider their specificity versus summary quality. How many of your memories can you tie to a specific moment in time? How many have distinct images that take you back to the precise events of the memory? How many memories are blends of similar events over time that cannot be traced to one single instance? How many convey more general ideas or feelings, but lack connection to a specific time or unique event?

5. **Settings and ending patterns:** Think about the way each chapter of your story ends. Think about how the majority of your memories end. Do your chapters and individual memories tend to end in a more upbeat or hopeful manner? Do these endings suggest the possibility of growth, improvement, greater understanding, or happiness ahead? Or do your endings strike a tone of resignation, frustration, anger, or resentment? How indeed do the stories within your story turn out, and how do you see the ultimate end of your life story—as one filled with integrity and hope or confusion and despair?

6. **Patterns of meaning-making:** Now consider the various messages, lessons, and morals you have drawn or might draw from your life story. Look over the theme that you assigned to sum up your overarching life story. Then look at any lesson statements that you have linked to your key episodes and self-defining memories. Do you indeed tend to step back and draw connections or messages from the remembered experiences of your life? Does this kind of reflection and rumination over life events come naturally or awkwardly to you? Make note also of all memories from which you have not drawn a particular lesson. We will return to these memories later on. It stands to reason that if you have recalled a memory as a key episode or a self-defining memory, it must have some greater significance for you, even if you have not as yet articulated explicitly what that significance is.

UNDERSTANDING AND CHANGING YOUR LIFE STORY

You have now gathered a wealth of information to answer the question that began this chapter: Who are you? You have at your disposal all the components of your life story—the primary device that individuals living in our society employ to craft a sense of identity.

In encouraging you to step back and look at the patterns within your life story, I am also urging you to find meanings and perhaps traps that may be hidden from superficial view. These traps can consist of repeated emotional sequences or "scripts" that operate in a fairly automatic fashion. In some cases, we may act on these scripts without being aware of their self-defeating aspects. Clearly, this was the case for my client Carl with regard to his outbursts of anger and manipulative behaviors in response to threats to his sense of adequacy.

In the last sections of this chapter, I address three aspects of your life story in which you can make concrete interventions in order to work toward a healthier life story and sense of identity. These three aspects are:

- Changing scripts

- Finding specificity in your memories

- Finding more meaning in your memories

Changing Scripts

One of the hardest things to do in all of human behavior is to break a self-defeating pattern of emotional responses. Most of my work as a therapist involves helping people to identify these patterns and then assisting them in the slow struggle to extract themselves from these repetitive and painful cycles. I realize that in recommending the life story exercises from this chapter, I have only provided a small first step in the daunting task of putting an end to a self-defeating script. However, I do believe that greater awareness and monitoring of the moments when a script emerges are invaluable stops along the way toward freedom from this constricting emotional trap. Some individuals find that once they have brought the beast out in the open and stared it eye to eye, the pattern tends to dissipate and go away on its own.

For those of you who are not so lucky, I urge you to write out the pattern you have identified in your memories. Trace out the sequence of your feelings and connect this sequence in the clearest terms to some of your key episodes and self-defining memories. When you have it fully in your sights and know your pattern well, you can then begin to consider alternative endings to the sequence that would bring you closer to what you want in life. This is exactly what Carl did when I asked him to define his wants.

Your first step then is to define for yourself clearly both what you want and what alternative actions would bring you closer to these goals. You can then use imagery and even role-playing (with a counselor or confidante) to rehearse your new response to the same old "hot buttons." It may not work every time, but any time it does work, the sense of accomplishment and elation at breaking the self-defeating cycle will be sure to inspire you to keep trying.

Ultimately, you may need the concentrated help of a counselor to break free from the most persistent scripts (particularly those that involve intimate interpersonal relationships). However, if you have done the prep work described in this chapter of reviewing your life story and breaking down your self-defeating patterns into their life story components, your counselor or therapist will have a great advantage in helping you attack the problem. With these life story components at your disposal, the therapeutic process to change your script should be greatly accelerated.

Finding Specificity in Your Memories

I have emphasized in this chapter that it is helpful for individuals to recall memories that are highly specific, filled with imagery, and traceable to a specific day and time. These recollections employ memory's full power to bring us back to the experience in question and grasp its full emotional significance for us. If you have found that your tendency is to recall memories in only more summary, and not imagistic, terms, I would like to make a few suggestions to help you in this process.

In the case of highly threatening or traumatic memories, your defenses may be helping you from becoming overwhelmed by the painful details of a horrible event in your life. If you notice that your memories are very vague or summarized for these kinds of events, I would urge you to go slow in looking for the details and to work together with a psychotherapist to guide the timing and appropriateness of more specific recall.

If you do notice that your memories are summarized for emotional events that are not in the category of traumatic experiences, then I can indeed recommend some exercises to sharpen the focus and specificity of your memories.

First, make use of the memory aids described earlier. Reviewing a letter, diary entry, photograph, or souvenir can serve to revive details of experiences that you thought were lost long ago.

Second, improving your memory for details is no different than methods to improve your dream recall. When students keep dream logs in my class, they find that by diligently asking themselves what they dreamt the minute they wake up and writing down the dream in a journal, their dream recall improves dramatically over two weeks. In the same way, if you take the time to write down a memory when it comes back to you in the course of the day along with whatever details are associated with that memory, you will find in a similar period of two weeks a dramatic sharpening of your memory for events in your life. Most memory connections from past events in your life have not disappeared, they are just dormant due to the lack of concentrated thought given to them.

Once you have developed a more enhanced memory recall, you will find that discussion of your memories will bring a richer palette of emotions to the surface. You will be able to feel past experiences from your life a bit more strongly and make clearer connections from these experiences to your current concerns. The research from my lab shows that the ability to make these connections is linked to your overall adjustment as well as more effective coping with experiences that present challenges or stress.

Finding More Meaning in Your Memory

The last intervention with regard to your life story is to find more lessons and messages from your key episodes and self-defining memories. There are two methods for doing this.

First, you must think of every one of your memories as a mini poem or haiku. It contains a metaphor that reflects something of meaning and import for your life. For example, I had one client who had a tortured relationship with his father. They could seldom communicate effectively and barely ever shared a word of affection. When my client's father lay in his hospital bed, he complained that he could not see the clock on the wall and never knew the time. My client went and bought him a clock to put on his table. His father died only a few weeks later. On the morning that he died, my client went to say his good-byes and found his father unconscious, no longer able to be revived. In his hands was the clock that his son had bought.

This memory has a basic emotional power—it tells us that his father treasured a gift from his son and held it close to him near the moment of his death. Yet the memory also has a metaphoric power that my client worked to find and then use in his life. My client saw this memory's metaphor in the following way:

> How do we use the time we are given with those we love? Do we squander it in petty conflicts? If we are unwise, will we be left clutching for that precious time when it is far too late?

I have chosen this particular memory because of its obvious symbolism and its vivid emotion, but all of our self-defining memories contain similar metaphors and meanings that are there to be deciphered. We must treat our memories not just as residues of past experiences, but also as symbolic expressions of our brain's efforts to construct and find meaning in the world.

Treat your memories as your own personal creative compositions and then do your best to find the most helpful and meaningful interpretations for your life.

A second, more concrete way to enhance your memory meaning-making is to try the following task. I asked you to take note of all of the key episodes and self-defining memories you have collected that do not have any kind of meaning-making statement associated with them. Now take each memory and apply the following phrase to it:

This memory has taught me that . . .

This simple exercise allows you in a very direct way to see what important lessons you tend to emphasize in your life story. It should also help you to become more adept and comfortable with this meaning extraction process. The German researcher Ursula Staudinger (2001) has repeatedly demonstrated that individuals whom others designate as particularly wise possess exactly this ability to step back and reflect on the meaning and implications of their life experiences.

CONCLUDING THOUGHTS

It may seem like it is much harder work for all of us living in contemporary society to define who we are than it has been for individuals from any previous eras. Instead of inheriting a set of clear roles and relationships that mark our social standing, religious affiliation, and familial prospects, we are personal novelists, writing lifelong sagas with interweaving themes, multiple characters, key episodes, and problematic endings. On top of that, we need to be personal critics, rereading the stories that we craft and then extracting themes, metaphors, and meanings from them. This may be fine for the English majors among us, but for everyone else, it seems like a huge headache.

And in a lot of ways it is. We hustle to carve out a niche that makes sense to us. We veer between accomplishments and connections, never sure of the optimal balance between agency and communion and what is best for our loved ones or us. We impose our own personal stereotypes and scripts on the people and interactions in our lives. Our personal efforts to make meaning can also trap others in our idiosyncratic view of the world. We may have found a way to define our individuality and identity, but we may inadvertently define others (whether they like it or not) along the way.

Despite all these difficulties, it is an exhilarating freedom to know that we can be the authors of our own identity. We can tilt at windmills, dance on the roofs of our apartment buildings, see ourselves as racecar drivers. We can love people of our same sex, live in a country far from home, marry a person from a different faith. In all that we do, we are writing our own unique stories, built from memories resonant with metaphors and meanings that connect and unite the varied chapters.

We are indeed works of art, fragile in our singular creations, born of chemical and synapse, highly susceptible to criticism and rejection, but somehow never yielding in our effort to write on the pages of the days that pass and will pass this one story that is our life.

4

Using Memories to Control Your Moods

Look around your office or your bedroom. Do you have pictures of family or friends on your desk or dresser? Do you have framed photographs from family vacations or posters from favorite art exhibits, films, or concerts hanging on your walls? Have you ever considered that these photographs and posters are ways to control your mood? When you look over at them during the course of your day, you are sparking positive memories associated with the people, places, and events depicted in their images. Work may be slow, the kids may be driving you crazy, but for the one moment that your eye makes contact with those sunlit orange canyons in Utah or takes in a circle of loving smiles from your wedding day, your mind transports you to a different place and time. You can live for just that instant in a serene place or a joyous celebration, and your spirits are lifted.

Psychologists call this exact experience the process of *mood regulation*. How mood regulation works and the role that memories play in sustaining good moods and repairing bad ones are the subjects of this chapter. We look at how individuals learn to draw on memories to control their moods and why depressed individuals have so much trouble doing this effectively. We meet Carolina, a woman suffering from depression, and learn how she gained better control over her memory in order to improve her mood. Finally, you will learn how to build your own "mood-memory repair kit" to maximize the positive and minimize the negative moods in your life.

THE MOOD-MEMORY CONNECTION

In the 1980s, the psychologist Gordon Bower, of Stanford University, made popular the term *mood congruency* to refer to the idea that we learn and recall information better when the emotion connected to that information (for example, happiness or sadness) agrees with our current mood (Bower 1981). Drawing on a humorous example from the silent film *City Lights*, with Charlie Chaplin, Bower described how a wealthy man who befriends the tramp played by Chaplin only remembers him when he has been drinking, but ignores him and humiliates him during his daytime sobriety. In other words, the rich man made a link between his current state (drunk or sober) and what he was able to remember (his relationship to the tramp). Extending this idea to mood and memory, Bower proposed that people also link their memories to moods, meaning that when a memory agrees in emotion with your current mood, you will be much more likely to remember it. In other words, people in happy moods should be more likely to remember happy memories, and people in sad moods should be more likely to remember sad memories. Our memories should be *congruent* with our moods.

To support this idea, Bower and his colleagues used hypnotic suggestion to get people into certain moods and then demonstrated that they remembered words that agreed with their suggested mood state better than those that did not. They also found the same agreement of mood and memory for childhood experiences and events recorded in a daily diary. These results inspired literally hundreds of subsequent studies by other researchers using a variety of ways to get laboratory participants into moods and then checking if their memories matched their moods.

The method of getting people into different moods is called *mood induction*, and psychologists have shown great ingenuity in inducing happy and sad moods in participants. Some play mournful slow music; others set up situations in actual stores or supermarkets where participants "win" free prizes or "find" money left behind. Participants watch film clips of sad scenes or listen to happy or sad stories. Sometimes, participants are asked to concentrate on a happy or sad image from their own life. Other times, participants read a series of statements on index cards with positive or negative emotion words on each card. The goal of all these mood induction techniques is to get people into a certain strong mood state and then see if their memories are likely to agree with the induced mood.

Mood Maintenance and Repair

After nearly twenty-five years of this research, we now have a clearer answer to Bower's original proposal about the agreement between mood and memory. He was right about positive moods, but less so about negative moods. The research has indeed supported his idea that individuals in happy moods are faster to recall happier memories and less likely to recall negative memories from their lives. However, research does not show such consistent agreement between negative moods and sad memories. Follow-up studies have not been able to show that the typical individual placed in a temporary bad mood will be more likely to recall sad memories.

Why isn't there agreement of mood and memory in both positive and negative moods? Many researchers, including myself, have pursued the answer to this question. The general consensus has led to a modification of Bower's mood congruency idea. This modification is called *mood maintenance and repair* (Isen 1985). The basic idea is that nondepressed individuals are motivated to *maintain positive moods* and *repair negative moods*. Healthy individuals are generally able to keep themselves in good spirits and a happy frame of mind; they know how to control their moods in an adaptive way.

Consider this example of mood maintenance: When things are going well, you let your mind play over the positive moments from your day, week, and more distant past. When you finish a project at work and are driving home satisfied, you let your mind wander to other successes from the past. You savor your feelings of accomplishment and embellish them with the glow of other victories and achievements. By the time you come through the front door, you are ready to give your husband a hug and greet the kids with an enthusiastic squeeze. You maintain your positive mood by using images and memories to sustain and enhance an already existing positive feeling.

Now you're driving home from a not-so-good day; the boss has yelled about a deadline, and your coworker took another sick day, leaving you with double duty on a report that is overdue. There is traffic, and the radio announces that the stock market plunged lower. As these events bombard you and you feel your mood sinking lower and lower, you start to think about the soccer game that your daughter played in the previous weekend. You can still see her ponytail flying as she made a breakaway down the field and managed with a bit of awkwardness to kick the winning goal for her team. You can remember her smiling, surprised face as her teammates and coaches nearly crushed her with hugs of celebration. You savor this memory from every angle, hearing the shouts of the excited parents, smelling the fall air, and letting your mind's eye luxuriate in the rich red color of the soccer uniforms and the backdrop of the green field and yellow-orange hills. By the time you pull into the driveway, you have put the day's struggles in their proper place and have shaken off the worst of your bad mood. Work frustrations are still there, but your mood is no longer moving in a negative direction. In fact, you feel eager to see your daughter and hear about her day. All in all, it should be a pretty good evening.

The ability to use memory to take you away from negative moods and bring you back to a more positive frame of mind is what we mean by mood repair.

When researchers first found that they couldn't show agreement between negative moods and sad memories for the typical individual, my colleague Peter Salovey and I argued that this might be because nondepressed individuals would find little value in hanging on to bad moods through dwelling on unhappy memories from the past. It would make more sense that individuals would want to work their way out of this negative space and into a more positive frame of mind. To support our point, we found that when studies did show agreement between negative moods and sad memories, they were almost always studies of individuals who suffered from anxiety and depression. Even more, when you looked closely at these studies, the results tended to show not that depressed individuals in bad moods recalled more sad memories, but in fact that they tended to recall fewer happy memories or were slower in recalling happy memories. So these results even deepened our ideas about mood repair.

We concluded that Bower's mood congruency idea did not hold up for nondepressed people because these individuals rely on positive memories and other positive thoughts to get them out of bad moods (mood repair). They may find that a bad mood brings them initially to sad thoughts or memories, but they then counteract these negative thoughts with more positive images and memories. On the other hand, depressed individuals are less successful in recruiting positive memories to overcome their negative moods. The result is that they show more agreement between their negative moods and subsequent memories. As a consequence, they are more likely to stay stuck in their bad moods.

Having proposed this idea, we set out to find support for it through a laboratory study. Working with our colleague Braden Josephson (Josephson, Singer, and Salovey 1996), we set up the following experiment: Using a depression screening inventory, we were able to identify two groups of depressed versus nondepressed undergraduate students. The depressed students tended to be in the mild to moderate range of depression. Few of them were clinically depressed or required medication, but they still scored much sadder than the average undergraduate. We then showed the two groups an edited set of scenes from the film *Terms of Endearment* (with Jack Nicholson, Shirley MacLaine, and Debra Winger), about a young mother who dies of cancer. After watching the film, the participants wrote down two memories from their lives.

Based on the mood repair hypothesis, we predicted that nondepressed individuals would first write down a negative memory (due to the sad film clip), but then follow it with a positive memory in order to repair their mood. On the other hand, individuals with higher depression scores would be more likely to write down two consecutive negative memories and not engage in mood repair.

This was exactly what we found. Participants who had two negative memories in a row had almost double the depression scores of participants who followed a negative memory with a positive one. When we asked the nondepressed individuals why they had recalled a second memory that was more positive than the first, over 60 percent of them said that they did not want to stay in a sad mood after having viewed the painful film clip. They wrote down statements like, "I wanted to think about something happier in order to lift my spirits."

Depression and Mood Repair Problems

Why do depressed individuals struggle with repairing bad moods? Researchers and clinicians have proposed a variety of answers to this question. One possibility is that depression undermines mental energy, and it takes more effort to find a memory that goes against your current mood.

Memory consists of networks of connected associations in your brain. Some associations are easier to find than others. For example, if I say the word "sauce" and then ask you to think of a fruit, you will be much more likely to say "apple" than "orange." This is an example of what psychologists call a "prime," something that has the power to inspire a connection between two associated words or ideas. The connection between "apple" and "sauce" makes it easier to think of one word when you say the other.

So for people in bad moods, finding associations to negative thoughts, memories, and images should be automatic and require minimal effort, while coming up with positive ideas and memories would mean more work. In other words, the bad mood primes related negative information. Nondepressed individuals have the energy and persistence to overcome this automatic reaction and look for the positive memory that will overcome the negative tendency. Depressed individuals, depleted by their illness, lack this mental muscle to bypass their easy negative associations and get to the more positive and mood-repairing memories.

This energy explanation may help to account for the problem, but there is some evidence that it does not explain the whole story. Some researchers have found that even after individuals have been on anti-depressants for a while and show improved mood and energy levels, they still have trouble recalling positive memories and, in particular, very detailed and specific positive memories.

This problem with recall of specific positive memories connects to a second major idea about why depressed individuals may have trouble with mood repair—depressed individuals tend to recall memories that are vague and overgeneral. These nonspecific memories lack vivid imagery and often cannot be linked to a specific day or moment in time. A researcher in the United Kingdom, Mark Williams (1996), first noted this phenomenon in the 1980s in a study of people who had attempted suicide, and it has been replicated many times since. Depressed individuals have trouble recalling specific memories and, in particular, specific positive memories. They take longer than nondepressed individuals to find specific memories of single events and are more likely not to find them at all.

Williams has theorized that this overgeneral memory style may have grown out of habits individuals learned very early in life to avoid threatening or unpleasant experiences. If depressed individuals faced a large number of negative events during their early childhood (such as deaths, separations, angry parenting, violent surroundings, and so on), they might have learned to block these painful moments out by not focusing on threatening details or images. What began as a strategy to avoid these negative experiences might then have generalized to a basic style of handling any kind of information. Individuals would simply keep all events at a vague general distance, protecting themselves against engaging with the details of any experience (of course, one would also lose the precious details of positive events).

In my own work I have not been able to show this overgeneral memory style for all memories in depressed individuals, but I have been able to find it in the positive memories of depressed individuals. Working with colleagues from my laboratory (Moffitt et al., 1994), we identified a group of depressed versus nondepressed undergraduate students and asked them to recall either a positive or negative memory and write it down. We then rated each memory as specific or general.

A specific memory would be "I remember the time that I hit my one and only home run in the Little League championship game and circled the bases while my dad waved to me from the stands."

A general memory would be "Growing up, I loved having my dad come to my ball games. He always stood up in the stands and would wave to me if I got a hit."

After we rated the memories, we first found that there was no difference in the depressed versus nondepressed group with regard to their detailed, specific negative memories; they both had roughly the same number. However, the depressed individuals had fewer specific positive memories than the nondepressed individuals. They indeed lacked a crucial ability to cheer themselves up with a specific positive memory when they were feeling down.

Based on these results, we can combine our thoughts about depressed individuals' lack of energy and their overgeneral memories and come up with a third possibility. Williams has argued that depressed individuals simply get stuck in their efforts to search through memory. As you might recall from chapter 1, we organize our memories in a kind of filing system. When we go to retrieve a memory, we start with a general heading or category (my years of college), we then look for a typical activity during that general time period (studying in the library), and then we locate within that activity a specific unique event (the time I fell asleep studying and the security guard had to wake me in order to close the library).

To get to this specific event with clear images and detail takes work. When the memory you are seeking to retrieve does not match your current mood state, this mismatch only increases the effort involved to move from a general level of memory to a more specific one. The result is that the depressed individual may indeed get stuck at a too general level of memory, especially for positive memories.

If this "getting stuck" problem is the main obstacle for depressed individuals in changing their negative moods, then couldn't therapists take a number of immediate steps to help them? For severely depressed individuals, antidepressants would assist them in rebuilding their energy levels and motivation, allowing them to make the extra effort to locate helpful specific memories. Additionally, one could aid individuals in writing down or rehearsing some of the specific positive memories that they do recall. By preparing ahead of time, individuals could overcome the tendency to get stuck at the general level of memory. Using cognitive behavioral techniques, therapists could also assist individuals with strategies for reorganizing their way of thinking, so that they would make more positive associations to situations, themselves, and others. By making these positive associations more common, they should become more available and easier to retrieve from memory.

Worry, Worry, Worry

All of these strategies—medication, rehearsing positive memories, increasing positive associations and experiences—potentially provide an antidote for the struggles of depressed individuals to succeed in mood repair. Yet there is still another problem that could threaten to sabotage all of these efforts. All of us, but particularly individuals prone to depression and anxiety, can get stuck in thought cycles where we worry and brood over the negative aspects of situations. We turn the focus of our thoughts to ourselves and, unfortunately, only direct the spotlight to the negative aspects of our current situation. If we start to think about our current relationship, we zero in on the conflicts and flaws in our partner, as well as the moments when we are least satisfied.

All the good gets pushed to the periphery, and we worry, worry, worry about all that is wrong.

Psychologists call this *rumination* and it is clearly linked to depression. It can also undercut efforts to identify and focus on positive memories (Lyubomirsky, Caldwell, and Nolen-Hoeksema 1998; Nolen-Hoeksema 2000). When we ruminate, we tend to see what is wrong with ourselves ("I can't do anything right"), focus excessively on our negative feelings ("I really can't shake these blues"), and obsess about the consequences of our depressed state ("As long as I am like this, no one is ever going to love me").

What are the consequences of rumination for memory and mood? Nolen-Hoeksema and her colleagues have found that depressed individuals who ruminate tend to recall more negative memories, rate them as more unhappy, and find it harder to recall positive memories. What all this means is that if you are stewing about the negatives in your life, looking to the past is only going to stir the pot and make things worse. Far from being able to repair their moods, ruminators who are already down can worsen their mood. Nolen-Hoeksema has even found that these depressed ruminators have trouble benefiting from friends or family who try to help. Their endless worrying and self-focused concerns eventually wear out well-meaning supporters ("No matter how many positives I see in you, you refuse to believe a word I say").

Luckily, these same researchers identified a positive strategy that can help shake these negative moods. Breaking the focus on oneself is the healthiest antidote to the ruminating blues. Thinking about a positive activity or another person, and simply doing things that preempt the thought process are steps that break the worry cycle. Unless depressed individuals break this cycle, it is unlikely that instructions to think about positive memories will be enough to pull them out of their negative moods.

Two German researchers (Joorman and Siemer, 2004) demonstrated exactly this point. Working with mildly depressed college students, they showed them a film clip of scenes from *Dead Poets Society* involving a student's suicide. The students were then asked to think about positive memories or to distract themselves by thinking about a shopping trip. Only the depressed students who distracted themselves saw any positive change in their mood. So the bottom line is that we can't simply tell depressed individuals to think about happy memories and expect a lift in mood. We have to intervene and stop the worrying cycle first, and then individuals may indeed gain benefits from concentrating on positive memories.

Recommendations Based on Memory and Mood Research

Putting all of these research advances on mood and memory together, here are some critical suggestions for how to be a good mood repairer:

1. Keep your mental and physical energy at good, healthy levels.

2. Arrange your immediate environments (bedroom, kitchen, workplace, study) in ways that make it easier for you to access positive, specific memories.

3. Take steps to increase your store of positive memories filled with specific images and concrete evidence of good things in your life.

4. Distract yourself from worries and negative thoughts.

5. Once you break the worry cycle, focus on the positive aspects of your experiences and memories.

Now these may sound like reasonable and straightforward steps to individuals who have never struggled with being depressed, but for those who are prone to depression, these five recommendations may feel overwhelming. In order to demonstrate how one can break them down into clear and manageable actions, let me share with you my experience working with Carolina.

HOW TO GET OFF THE WORRY CYCLE AND PUT A NEW SPIN ON YOUR LIFE

Carolina, an attractive freelance journalist in her forties, came to see me for a lingering depression. She had been severely depressed for several months and had found some relief from an antidepressant. After a few months of medication, she had resumed her previous work schedule and taken up almost all of her old routine. However, she still found herself stuck in a negative cycle of self-critical thoughts and waves of sadness that would overtake her and leave her feeling hopeless and defeated.

When I asked about some of the background to her depressed feelings, she traced them to a combination of stagnation in her career and ambivalence over her relationship with her current boyfriend. She had felt her writing career was in a rut due to her being typed as a writer on "women's health." She had longed to write about a wider spectrum of concerns—the natural world, travel, politics, but found it hard to land these assignments. As for her boyfriend, she knew that she was clear about not marrying him (she had been married once before and had no interest in getting remarried), but had felt intense pressure from him to go this route. By the time I met Carolina, she had made great progress on both of these fronts. She had begun a series of travel pieces and had recently returned from a tour of the Canadian Rockies and Lake Louise. She had also moved on from her boyfriend and felt both freedom and relief that she had not committed herself to a huge mistake.

What Carolina wanted to know from me was, Why didn't she feel better and why did her mind continue to race with negative thoughts and memories? She was taking her meds and had made positive concrete changes in her life, but she still sat in bed at night and worried herself awake all night. When I asked her about what happened when she tried to think more positively, she emphasized that every doctor she had ever talked to asked about trying affirmations and using more positive thinking. The problem was that once she was alone with her thoughts, she found her memories would go back to the "wasted time" she had spent on articles that no longer interested her, or ways in which she may have hurt her ex-boyfriend or failed to give him clear messages. These memories would only remind her of earlier memories—of how she should have majored in English instead of being pre-med or how she had agreed to marry her ex-husband when she knew in her heart that she did not want to be married.

Having taken all this history, I realized that there were many complicated and deep therapeutic issues to address, and that we would have much work to do together (see Singer, 2005 for a discussion of person-based therapy and a multidimensional approach to treatment), but I also set an immediate and concrete goal to work on her very specific problem of getting trapped in down moods. I explained to Carolina that as part of an overall therapy I would like to help her learn how to use her memories to become better at changing bad moods and maintaining positive ones.

In order to do this, we would need to take a series of steps. The first one was to have her take pictures of the walls, desktops, and table surfaces of her bedroom and office. The second was to write down a list of her five most positive memories. The third was to write down two of her most negative memories. The fourth was to bring in a list of current or potential activities that would give her pleasure and potentially distract her thoughts.

Carolina was used to taking photographs to illustrate her articles, and she had no problem sending me digital photographs over the Internet that portrayed the ways in which she decorated her familiar spaces. She struggled a bit more with writing down five positive memories, but was able to bring in a rather cursory and vague list. I teased her that as a writer she might have provided a bit more detail and color, but she should not worry because we could consider this list her first draft. She had less trouble writing down her two negative memories in a bit more detail (one concerning the day she spent at court awaiting her divorce decree, and the other sitting through her organic chemistry final and knowing that she was flunking it and would never be a doctor). Finally, she brought in a list of more positive activities and indicated how surprised she was with the large number she had generated.

With all these valuable materials assembled, we were ready to go to work. First, we looked carefully at the photograph of her living space. Carolina had some very attractive abstract prints on her bedroom wall, a few plants, photographs of her parents, and a jewelry box along with a hairbrush on her dresser. When she sat in bed at night reading, this was what she would see from her pillow.

I asked her what memories she associated with each of these objects. As Carolina described memories connected to the prints, she revealed that she had bought one of them with her ex-husband and the more recent one at a gallery she visited with her now ex-boyfriend. When we talked about the photograph of her parents, she described a memory of her father's disappointment with her when she announced that she would not be applying to medical school. I asked about the jewelry box, and she mentioned that her best friend from high school and college years, Carrie, had given it to her. She still felt a strong connection to Carrie, but had hardly been in touch with her over the last few years, especially this past year during her bout with depression.

Finally, I asked about the hairbrush, and she told me that she had been given it by one of the women's cosmetic companies that she had covered for a story about aging skin.

It was not hard to see problems with each of these decoration choices. As much as she liked the prints, each one was associated with a flood of negative memories about the two men who had accompanied her when she purchased them. Although she felt an obligation to have a picture of her parents on her wall, looking at it at this particular juncture of her life was not bringing happy memories or positive associations to mind. The jewelry box had the potential to bring happy memories of Carrie to mind, but only if she took some action to bring her connection to Carrie back to life. The hairbrush only served to stir up subtle reminders of the type of article she no longer wanted to write.

Mood-Memory Makeover

So our goal was now to do a *mood-memory makeover*. Just like those reality television shows where people redo their dens or get consultation on their wardrobe, our goal was to redecorate her bedroom to maximize the possibilities that memories filled with more positive specific images would be likely to come to mind. We agreed that the prints would come down, and in their place a picture from her recent trip to the Rockies would go up.

Next, the photograph of her parents would be moved to another place in the bedroom that was not in her line of vision from her pillow. In the place of her parents, she would put a picture of her schnauzer, Lulu, who was a source of constant and undying positive love. Lulu, who slept on the pillow next to Carolina, would certainly appreciate this new canine view. The jewelry box would stay where it was, but Carolina needed to make a commitment to call Carrie and share a positive conversation. She resisted this, but finally called and had a warm and reaffirming talk. So next to the jewelry box went a picture of Carrie and Carolina dressed for the prom in high school. Finally, the brush and all its connections to magazine articles she now detested went in the drawer and stayed there. A new brush, bought with pleasure at her favorite salon, took its place.

Carolina's Bedroom Mood-Memory Makeover	
Before	**After**
Two prints (one bought with ex-husband, one with ex-boyfriend)	Rockies photo (represents new life)
Parents' photograph (brings back criticisms)	Pet photo (current companion)
Jewelry box (gift from best friend who has grown out of touch)	Box stays but add photo of friend (keeps connection to friend more alive)
Hairbrush (reminds her of hated work)	New hairbrush (reminds her of new life)
Result: Continual associations to negative memories	**Result:** Surrounding herself with positive associations and memories

With Carolina's physical space in order (we also did the same makeover to her office decor), we turned to her list of positive memories. Using some of the techniques described earlier in this book, I helped Carolina to develop more powerful imagery and detail for each of the positive memories she had listed. These memories included receiving her first schnauzer as a child (Lulu's great-great-grandmother), seeing her first article in print in a national magazine, swimming with the dolphins on a tropical vacation, and eating at a four-star restaurant in Paris. We worked on her ability to savor and visualize these memories until they could be considered her *go-to memories*. By this I mean that she could know that these memories were available and ready to be visualized when she needed to soothe herself or lift her spirits.

Carolina's Go-To Memories

1. First schnauzer

2. First national magazine article

3. Swimming with dolphins

4. Restaurant in Paris

Next, we looked at her two strong negative memories, the memory of sitting in divorce court and the other memory of flunking her exam. Our goal in this work was to see if we could identify *positive* aspects of both of these memories. Carolina first thought this would be impossible, but then realized that each memory was as much about freedom as it was about failure. Her day in divorce court ultimately represented liberation from a marriage that she should never have entered. Similarly, her flunking organic chemistry could now be seen as a step away from a path that her father had wanted for her, but that in her heart was not what she truly wanted. So in a strange way, if she looked at it from the right angle, both memories offered positives in her life. Acknowledging these factors was far from seeing these memories as *good* memories, but seeing their positive aspects was a way to neutralize the pain or sadness they brought back when they were recalled. These memories were striking examples of how Carolina could turn other "lemon memories" in her life to "lemonade."

Carolina's Lemons-into-Lemonade Memories

1. Sense of shame at divorce court   ⇒   Freedom from bad marriage

2. Failing organic chemistry exam   ⇒   Freedom from pressure to be a doctor

---

Finally, all of the above work would be to no avail if we could not break Carolina's cycle of ruminations. How could we stop her from going down that slope of finding fault, focusing on how bad it feels to find fault, and then ultimately giving in to a rush of despair? Based on the research discussed above, the answer lay in teaching her to distract herself from rumination. This is where her list of potential pleasant activities came in. As we went over the list, we evaluated which ones she thought might be most possible. After a lot of "yes, buts . . ." ("Yes, but" is the familiar protection of the depressed person whenever someone makes a positive suggestion—"Yes, that's a good suggestion, but . . ."), Carolina agreed to choose one activity that she would commit to trying.

After exploring what would fit her schedule, be most convenient, and disrupt Lulu's life the least, Carolina decided to try a spinning class at the health club two blocks from her house. Spinning is a kind of aerobic exercise that consists of riding a stationary bicycle as an instructor leads you through a workout. Carolina pointed out that the times when she was most likely to get into a negative thinking cycle were after work in the early evening and late at night in bed. Spinning classes met two nights a week after dinner and tired her out so that she was able to take a bath and get a good night's sleep. She found that with the music and the instructor's commands there was little time for rumination.

Carolina's List of Positive Activities

1. Attending dog shows

2. Joining a book group

3. Joining a writers' group

4. Taking a cooking class

5. Spinning

6. Taking a dance class

7. Taking a graduate course

8. Making bread with friends

Of course, we explored many other concerns in Carolina's life that did not lend themselves to a set of clear exercises. Yet for this one problem of learning how to stop the downward cycle of negative moods, our series of interventions was highly effective. They were simple steps to protect her from the daily hassles of life and the subtle ways in which the world around her or inside her could sneak up and take hold of her mood. Even if big matters in Carolina's life were yet to be resolved, we had succeeded in fortifying her against some of the more irritating and debilitating little ones.

YOUR MOOD-MEMORY REPAIR KIT

Now we can put some of the lessons we have discussed about memory and mood to work in your life. You are going to assemble your own mood-memory repair kit that will be available to raise your mood and protect you from ruminations that can drag you down. You will want to get out your memory journal as a place to write down some of the information requested in your mood-memory repair kit. Table 3 lists the features of your mood-memory repair kit.

Table 3: Your Mood-Memory Repair Kit

1. **Mood-memory makeover list:** a survey of your bedroom, office, and other important rooms for any objects that evoke negative memories

2. **Go-to memories:** five positive memories that can be counted on to pick up your spirits

3. **Lemons-into-lemonade memories:** two negative memories that have some positive aspects

4. **Positive distracting activities:** a list of distractions to break the cycle of rumination and worry

Mood Accessories (At No Extra Charge!):

5. **Surefire pick-me-up lines:** key phrases to prime positive memories

6. **The don't-go-there rubber band:** traditional thought-stopping technique

7. **Nose candy:** smells that evoke positive memories

Your Mood-Memory Makeover

To conduct your mood-memory makeover, you should choose a single room (you can add more later) to survey for any possible negative reminders. It can help to photograph the areas in order to step back from the space and also to discuss it with someone who has not seen the decorations before. By talking with someone else about the decorations in the photographs, you are forced to explain their origins and inevitably will find the associated memories surfacing. This exercise should give you real insight into what subtle negative associations you are experiencing within a setting that is supposed to be supportive and reinforcing of your positive energy.

Your Go-To Memories

In making up your list of go-to memories, keep in mind that you might want to be able to recruit different types of positive memories for different circumstances. For this reason it might be helpful to have positive academic, family, athletic, and work experiences, and so on. Once you have discussed, visualized, and truly stored these strong positive experiences, you can selectively draw on them to remind you of your successes or positive relationships at junctures when negative memories in these areas threaten to pull you down.

Your Lemons-into-Lemonade Memories

The purpose of lemons-into-lemonade memories is to prove to yourself that these memories not only will not defeat you, but that they have opened doors or have been catalysts for change in your life. Begin with two examples from your life where a negative experience became an opportunity for learning. You may identify a personal setback or failure; you may think of a loss or conflict. You may come up with a moment of shame or humiliation, including attacks on your heritage, religion, or race. In each of the cases that you select, your goal is to articulate the meaning and value that emerged from the experience. In other words, try to define how it changed you for the better. Once you have this in mind, you must make sure that this connection becomes a permanent part of the memory. It might help to write down the memories in your journal, using the format for collecting self-defining memories described in chapter 2 (describe the memory in as vivid terms as you can, but add the phrase, "This memory has taught me . . .). Make sure to emphasize the positive lesson you have gained. Though you have started with two, you should continue to seek these positive angles in other, more difficult memories. By changing the way that you see the ultimate value and purpose of a memory, you can go a long way toward reducing its pain and your tendency to ruminate on its negative aspects excessively.

By changing the way that you see the ultimate
value and purpose of a memory, you can go a long
way toward reducing its pain and your tendency to
ruminate on its negative aspects excessively.

Your Positive Distracting Activities

With your memories under greater control and ready to be
recruited for mood repair, we must also ensure that ruminations don't
take hold and prevent you from using your mood-memory kit effectively. You can use positive distracting activities as healthy diversions
from excessive thinking about and second-guessing of past behaviors
and current difficult choices. You need to pick activities that take the
focus off you. When your mood starts to shift downward, consider it a
major alarm that you need to take up your distraction before your
worries are off and running. Use your positive activity list to select the
activities that are most convenient, that you are most likely to enjoy,
and that you will follow through on. Don't try to add too many new
distractions at a time. Start with one, and as you built it into your
regular routine, you can move on to a second or third.

Your Mood Accessories

At "no extra charge," I have added three accessory aids to your
mood-memory repair kit. They are meant to be extra means of support
to catch you if you start to slip into a more negative memory cycle.
First, surefire pick-me-up lines are quick phrases that you can use to
prime or cue your positive memory and activate its images. If you find
yourself starting to think negatively, you can simply say "Remember the
. . ." and the word associated with your memory can bring back the
images and events that lead to positive feelings. (Carolina used to say
to herself "Remember the dolphins" as a way of invoking her relaxing
and joyous memory of swimming with the dolphins.)

Cognitive behavioral therapists have long relied on the thought-
stopping technique of wearing a rubber band and giving yourself a
reminding snap on the wrist when your thoughts go in an unwanted
direction. So many of my recent clients are wearing colored bands to
support various humanitarian causes that this is indeed an easy (and

fashionable) accessory to add to the mix. When the negative thought begins, give yourself a quick (and discreet) snap from your don't-go-there band and then immediately recite your surefire pick-me-up lines.

Finally, it is well-known that smell has powerful connections to memory. In the great novel of memory, Marcel Proust's *Remembrance of Things Past*, the smell of a tea-soaked madeleine brings back in vivid photographic detail the entire world of a childhood village left long ago. A woman's perfume as she passes on the street can break your heart by reminding you of someone that you loved and lost twenty years earlier. The smell of fried onions on the burner can take you immediately to Sunday breakfasts prepared by your mother and the warm lazy feeling of lying in your bed while you waited to be called down to the table.

The power of smell is closely linked to emotion. Of all the nerve cell connections between your sensory organs and your brain, the connection between the olfactory receptors in your nose and the olfactory cortex in your brain is the most direct. Smell receptors pick up odors and send their chemical information to the olfactory bulb, which lies close to the midbrain or limbic area, the part of the brain most associated with emotion. The olfactory bulb sends that information on to the olfactory cortex, which translates that chemical information into perceptual information that can be identified with specific memories and odor labels.

So it makes sense to add smells to your mood-memory repair kit. What you want to do is make a list in your memory journal of smells that hold associations to positive memories for you. For example, many men that I have talked to over the years have very positive associations to the smell of the oil used to soften a new baseball mitt. As Little Leaguers, part of their spring ritual with a new glove was to put the softening oil on the stiff new glove with a ball tied inside it and let the glove take shape over a few days. Now as adults even the slightest whiff of that old smell brings back to these men elaborate memories of getting into their uniform, stepping on the ball field grass, and buying hot dogs from the snack stand after the game.

Once you have your personal list, see if you can put together a little smell chest of your positive smells. Many women find these scents (such as vanilla, sandalwood, tea rose, China rain, and so on) in bubble baths, scented candles, or body washes. Men recall the aftershaves used by their fathers or cigars enjoyed by their grandfathers on the front porch on a summer night. Keep your supplies of these memory makers handy and when a negative mood threatens, fill the bath, light the candle, or open the box where you keep the cigars. Take in the smell and then let your mind drift to this positive and soothing place in your memory.

CONCLUDING THOUGHTS

In this chapter I have argued that you do not need to be a slave to bad moods. You can take control of moments when you start to drift into a negative frame of mind, and your own memories can be your best ally in stopping this drift. Individuals not inclined to depression know this trick instinctively and make use of positive memories all the time to repair moods when they start to feel blue. However, some of us need more help in this regard and that is where the mood-memory repair kit fits in. Using the suggestions in this kit, you have several concrete steps to take that will help fortify you against the downward slide of negative moods. By working to identify positive memories, but also by ensuring that you build positive distractions into your life, you will be much better prepared to get off the downward cycle and join Carolina in putting a new, more positive spin on your life.

5

Memories and Loss

In the previous chapter we learned about methods to control negative moods through focusing on positive memories, but what about when your mood goes far beyond a blue feeling to deep sorrow and pain? What role can memories play when you have suffered a major loss in your life? Where do memories fit in when you have lost a loved one? The goal of this chapter is to recognize both the power of memory in facing these losses and its role in helping you to move forward from these difficult transitions. You will learn how to preserve memories, but also how to take steps to resume your life instead of allowing your grief to overwhelm and paralyze you. How indeed might we make memory our ally and teacher rather than an enemy that wounds us with sorrow and regret?

ONE MAN'S GRIEF

Roberto was a good family man in his midfifties. He had raised two fine sons who were launched on their own careers and families. He enjoyed his wife, Sue, and liked his job as an accountant for a major insurance firm. However, his father, who had been in reasonably good health, suddenly succumbed to a stroke and died at age seventy-eight. First, the news floored Roberto like the stab of a knife and then, as he was swept up in all the busy details that surround a death, he felt numb. Friends and coworkers were very sensitive to him and he felt an outpouring of love and support. A couple of weeks passed and he resumed work. Though most people around him settled back into their routines and no longer checked in with him about his grief, Roberto continued to find great comfort from his family. They talked openly about missing Grandpa and the hole his death had left in their lives.

After six months or so, Roberto felt that he really should not dwell much more on his loss; even his family seemed to have moved on and made little reference to the death. When he called his sister or brother and brought up the subject, they sympathized with his sadness but quickly changed the subject. He felt like he was getting the message from all around him that the appropriate period of grieving had passed and it would seem almost morbid to keep bringing up memories or thoughts about his dad.

The problem was that he would find himself sitting at his desk at work and tears would well up. He would sneak off to the men's room and lock himself in a stall and quietly cry. When one of his sons would call to tell him about something his newborn grandson had done, he would find himself thinking back to times with his own father and he would no longer be able to absorb what his son was saying. Once he was in the hardware store and an older man walked in wearing the same Old Spice aftershave that his father used to wear, and he had to hide in a corner of the store to avoid anyone spotting his tears.

Roberto wasn't sure what to do about his feelings and in particular the vivid memories of his father that seemed to grab hold of his chest and leave him with a sharp ache in his heart. He could recall the tap of his father's razor on the sink as he got ready for work each morning, his father's whistle to their family dog when it was time for the evening walk, his father's constant presence at his basketball games and cross-country meets.

Some of his most powerful memories were of runs they had taken together and how they would go to the local restaurant for Sunday breakfast after the run. His father would take down his mug from the peg on the wall reserved for regulars and pour himself a big cup of coffee while he laid out the Sunday *Times* on the table for them to read together. Roberto would never forget the morning when he turned seventeen: His father had told him to get his mug down from the wall for him, and there was one with Roberto's name on the peg next to his father's.

The problem was that these loving memories of his father seemed only to bring him pain rather than joy. It was like each memory brought him into a room that was warm and lit by firelight. He would settle comfortably into the memory and then a trapdoor would open and he would fall down a tube in darkness, his head dizzy, his heart racing, and his stomach queasy. Each memory ended with the simple crashing idea that his father was gone and would never be there again to share a joke, give a hug, or reassure him at a moment of doubt.

Roberto wasn't the kind of person who wanted to go to support groups or go on about himself to a counselor, though his wife encouraged him to try both of these aids. Ultimately, after talking with his minister, he decided to come and see me for help with his unremitting grief. Roberto found it a great relief to talk and indeed began to feel a bit better. The waves of sorrow lessened and he was able to function better at work and get back some of his spark. Still, his memories persisted and the question remained, How might he handle these difficult recollections that provoked such pain in his life?

To answer this question, we need to consider several aspects about the role that memory plays in loss. From there, we can see the concrete steps Roberto took to honor his memories, but also place them in a perspective that allowed him to overcome his sorrow.

MEMORIES AND COMPLICATED GRIEF

Recently, psychologists have paid great attention to the problem of "complicated grief" (Hasley et al. 2003). Complicated grief is the name for persistent intense grief that lasts for longer than six to twelve months after the loss of the loved one occurred. Individuals struggling with complicated grief have trouble speaking about their loss without bouts of intense sorrow or despair. They may sleep too much or too little; they may lose their appetite or overeat to soothe themselves. They may focus excessively on death and loss, bringing up the topic in almost every setting or conversation. Trivial frustrations or setbacks may instigate new outpourings of grief. Their work or usual activities may suffer, and their enjoyment of familiar activities may fade. Research has suggested that 15 percent of individuals who have suffered a major loss may indeed be at risk for major depression. Even if the complicated grief reaction does not escalate to a debilitating depression with thoughts of hopelessness and suicide, it can lead to increased abuse of drugs or alcohol and social withdrawal or conflict.

What causes complicated grief? Why do some individuals go through powerful periods of mourning but then move on effectively in their lives, while others seem to get stuck in a cycle of loss and sorrow? There are several factors that may contribute to the different responses to loss. Some people may have had a history of depression that was exacerbated by this new wave of pain. In some cases, the sudden or unexpected nature of the loss can leave a feeling of lack of resolution, confusion, or unanswered questions. Long-standing differences or conflicts with the lost loved one can cause the bereaved to wrestle with feelings of regret, resentment, or unfinished business. Even when there has been little conflict, a strong, dependent relationship with the departed person can lead to a lingering emptiness and disorientation. In other cases, for example, the loss of a child or a young sibling, one can be overwhelmed with feelings of guilt, injustice, and questions about faith or the ultimate meaning of life.

Regardless of the particular contributing factors to complicated grief, one of the powerful symptoms described by grieving individuals is the persistence of memories about the person they have lost. Suddenly, it seems that everywhere they turn there is a reminder of the deceased or a mention of death or loss that then floods them with memories. Just like in Roberto's case, their memories end up hurting more than soothing their hearts and minds.

It used to be believed that the solution to this problem was that individuals needed to "make their peace" with the loss by working through the loss to "gain closure." Much of grief counseling well into the 1990s worked toward the premise of resolving your grief and moving on. More recently, a new body of research has offered a different position on how to handle grief and the memories associated with loss.

NEW STRATEGIES IN HANDLING MEMORY AND GRIEF

The new wave of research on grief, led by John Harvey, George Bonnano, and Dennis Klass, among others, argues first, that there is no one path to handling grief, and second, that one should not necessarily seek to recover from or resolve one's loss. These researchers see bereavement as unique to each individual; each person's response expresses a complex reaction based on the relationship to the lost loved one, the circumstances of the loss, and the nature of the person who is bereaved. For a while it was fashionable to talk about a "time-line" or the "stages" of grief. Although these theories of how loss unfolds identified very important responses to loss, such as shock, denial, anger, depression, working through, and integration of the loss, the view that these responses proceed in some lockstep order is now seen as an oversimplification. Individuals show remarkable variation in their responses to loss.

Some will register only minimal overt grief and show no adverse effects from their limited response to what would appear to be a devastating loss. Others will tear their hair, rend their clothes, and wail until they are hoarse, but also show a healthy long-term response. What grief researchers and counselors have come to understand is that it is not only how you respond to the loss, but the eventual meaning and story that you construct about it that matters (Harvey 2002). In other words, what matters is how you incorporate the loss into your own sense of identity and life story. If you can do this in a positive fashion, you are likely to take your life forward, carrying the loss with you, but in a way that is best for your well-being and your relationships with others. If you can't find meaning out of the loss or can't allow it to become an instructive part of your own story, you are likely to remain caught up in its haunting images and the sorrowful emotions associated with them.

Returning to Roberto's problem of memory and loss, he clearly needed to find a way to take the recurrent memories that overwhelmed him and give them a meaningful place in his life's ongoing story. If he could see the memories that returned to him as leading somewhere rather than simply attacking his peace of mind, he would be more likely to take control of his grief and not allow it to paralyze him at work or home.

Once again, according to contemporary thinking about grief, his goal was not to stop thinking about his dad or end the grieving process. Rather, he needed to work toward the following five objectives (as outlined by Haley et al. 2003 and Harvey 2002):

1. Immediate symptom management

2. Making meaning out of the loss

3. Incorporating the lost one as an ongoing part of life

4. Using physical objects to keep the positive presence of the lost one in your surrounding environment

5. Embracing causes or values that were important to the lost one

Immediate Symptom Management

Roberto first had to address the acute physical and psychological symptoms associated with his powerful grief. Despite the legitimate pain he felt over his loss, it would do him little good in his professional life if one year after his father's death he were to begin to tear up or lose his concentration during an important quarterly meeting of his accounting group. He also needed to have a coping strategy to handle powerful memories that might overtake him in family situations when he was expected to be attentive to his wife or sons.

To work with him on this problem, I first used more general cognitive behavioral strategies (Meichenbaum 1994) that emphasize relaxation, thought stopping, and positive restructuring.

Roberto constantly referred to his body when he talked about his memories of his father. He described "aches in his chest," "dizziness," "waves of sadness," "feeling his hot tears," "loss of breath," and "weakness and fatigue." As a fundamental first step, we needed to break the learned connection that had emerged between his memories of his father and these negative physical states. After all, many of the memories that he recalled were of happy times and positive interactions with his father; therefore, it made little sense that they should now conjure up a host of negative physical symptoms associated with anxiety, panic, and depression.

As I outlined in chapter 2, I engaged Roberto in learning how to employ progressive muscle relaxation and imagery exercises. My goal was to get him to link images of his father that still caused pain with soothing and relaxing images that invoked calm and serenity. After a few weeks of practice, Roberto had reached a point where he could achieve a deep state of muscle relaxation and then focus on images of his father without increased anxiety or distress.

Similar to the thought-stopping intervention described in the previous chapter (the don't-go-there rubber band), I encouraged Roberto to wear a rubber band around his wrist for a few weeks as a protection against a negative turn in his thoughts. If he found memories of his father welling up and distracting him from pressing work or conversations, he needed to give his wrist a snap and then immediately call on one of his relaxing images to refocus his thoughts and attention.

We also emphasized in the last chapter the value of distraction. Another way Roberto could ensure symptom relief from the painful effects of his recurrent memories was to engage in positive distracting activities. At first, Roberto thought that jogging might be a big help in breaking his cycle of sadness and haunting memories. It turned out that going for a run reminded him so much of his dad that he would find himself quitting halfway and more upset than when he started. Leaving aside running, we tried a few different athletic activities and then settled on racquetball. Roberto found a friend from work for a weekly game, and the exercise and camaraderie did wonders for keeping his mind in a more positive and present-focused frame.

Making Meaning Out of Loss

Much of chapter 3's emphasis on memory and meaning argued that the key to the place of self-defining memories in our life stories is the lessons or insights that we might extract from them. This idea applies more to memories of loss than any other kind of memory. John Harvey and James Pennebaker (1995) have championed the position that the major "working through" that we must accomplish with grief is not to put our loss behind us, but to learn how to see it as part of our larger life story. Incorporating our grief in our ongoing story gives us the opportunity to find meaning from our sadness and to turn our pain into a lesson for life still ahead. Harvey (2002) calls this his "story-action" response to loss—we must both tell the story of our loss and then proceed with constructive action based on the legacy of the person we loved. As I pursued these ideas with Roberto, his persisting and disruptive sorrow over his father's death made a lot more sense.

In my conversations with Roberto, I started to gain some important insights into why he might indeed be suffering from a more prolonged or complicated grief. His father had been a quietly spiritual man, someone who had an abiding Christian faith that comforted him and organized his life. Roberto had never been able to share this aspect of his father's life and had secretly felt quite ashamed of his lack of sincere faith. Despite belonging to a church and raising his children to accept Christ and his teachings, Roberto had never felt a presence of God in his own life.

During the immediate days after his father's death, Roberto had relied on his minister for support and had spent a great deal of time in church for the memorial service and participating in prayers of remembrance. As the weeks and months accumulated, he began to feel a nagging feeling that he had let his father and his religion down. Here at this pivotal moment in his life, why couldn't he find in himself a greater sense of spiritual connection? Was he just a godless person or simply too shallow to feel the presence of a force larger than himself? He felt ashamed that he had not made this leap; he knew that his father would never have asked this of him, but somehow he saw himself as disappointing his father, as not carrying forward a positive legacy of faith. Ironically, when the most loving memories of his father would return to him, so would these gnawing and self-critical feelings about his ambivalence toward God.

To work more fully through these struggles, Roberto had joined a Bible study group at the church that shared readings and thoughts about scripture. As part of the group, each member took a turn sharing a "devotion" (a kind of mini sermon) with the larger congregation. When Roberto told me that his turn was coming up, I saw this as an excellent opportunity to connect the loss of his father to Harvey's story-action approach. I encouraged Roberto to write his devotion about his father.

At first Roberto questioned if he could do this. He felt that he did not deserve to talk about spiritual matters to the congregation when he saw himself as not preserving his father's unswerving faith. However, I encouraged him to just write about his father and what the loss of his father meant to him. As Roberto worked on writing out his thoughts, he began to see that his father's death had brought him closer to the church and then, even more, led him to join the Bible study. When he asked himself honestly why this had happened, he realized that this connection to his church was a way of holding on to an important bond with his father. The meaning he took from this was not to worry about the certainty of his belief at this time, but simply to continue the actions that made him feel closer to his father.

Roberto now saw his memories of his father in a new light. They were a way to keep his father alive in his heart, but they were also a way of taking tentative steps toward a deeper faith in God. The loss of his father was part of his own ongoing spiritual story. He shared these ideas, along with a few tears, with his fellow congregants, and they were very appreciative of his words. For Roberto this ability to express his sadness and see it as part of his personal struggle with faith made a great difference in his sorrow. The pain was still there and always would be, but now the memories were as likely to inspire as paralyze him. Now they reminded him of the link he was finding between love and faith, and he felt very grateful for this knowledge.

Incorporating and Preserving the Person in Your Life

As Roberto was beginning to feel more comfortable with the enduring images and memories of his father, I asked him how he might do something tangible to keep his father's presence in his life. Roberto suggested that he might ask his younger son, whose wife was pregnant, if he and his wife might consider giving their child a first or middle name that would honor his father. His name had been Luis, and so they could use this name or find a female variation including Louisa, Lucy, Luanne, or even Maria-Luisa. The couple was pleased to consider this possibility and when a boy was indeed born, they selected the name Lewis in honor of Roberto's father. Roberto was very happy about this way of keeping the presence of his father alive, and he loved to hold the baby and share memories of his father (Lewis's great-grandfather) while Lewis snuggled against his chest.

Keeping the Image of the Lost One in Your Physical Environment

As we discussed in the last chapter, physical objects, photographs, odors, and particular settings are all spurs to intense emotional memories. To keep memories of your lost loved one alive, you definitely would want to place photographs and mementos that are linked to that person in close and frequent sight. Roberto found a picture of his dad and him sitting in their local restaurant with the newspaper spread out in front of them. They were in their sweats and had clearly just finished their run. Roberto framed this photo and put it on the right edge of his desk. When he was writing up a report, on the phone, or scanning through his e-mail, he could see that picture and know how deeply valuable that time together was. Just a quick glance was enough to remind him of his commitment to his father's memory and the positive values he had instilled in him.

Embracing the Loved One's Values

Finally, Roberto felt that he needed to make his commitment to his father's memory more tangible. He needed to take action to perpetuate his father's faith and devotion to improving others' lives. Knowing how much his father had worked with his hands and built large parts of their family home, as well as how often his father had pitched in to swing a hammer for friends, Roberto decided that he would put what his father had taught him (both spiritually and physically) to work. He joined up with a Habitat for Humanity chapter and began to take some time each weekend to assist a family in putting up a new residence. He had never felt more connected to his dad since his death than during these hours of working alongside the group from the church and giving hard hours of physical labor for free. He truly enjoyed the people in the neighborhood and appreciated their assistance and contributions. The work for Habitat deepened his sense of meaning about his life while simultaneously giving a few more people a place to call home.

Converting Memories of Loss to Memories with Meaning

Roberto knew that the part of him inside that held the memories of his father's life would never fully "heal." It could not close up, grow new skin, and blend with the rest of his life. He was changed by his loss, perhaps permanently a bit sadder for this firsthand knowledge of grief, but he now also welcomed the additional depth of understanding he had gained from finding meaning in his memories. Where once they had only been a source of pain, now they were part of a larger story about the lessons that his father's life had taught him about love and faith. He was finally ready to "move on," but he was also moving in a new direction, a path that had been opened up by his loss. Now when the memories came of his father, of their runs together, of the tap-tap of the razor on the sink, or their mugs side by side at their breakfast place, he welcomed them not just as glimpses through the window of the past, but as a view forward of the new path his life had taken.

TAKING YOUR OWN STEPS TO BUILD MEMORIES OF MEANING FROM LOSS

You can also follow the steps that Roberto took to convert his memories of loss to memories of meaning. First, you should recognize that Roberto's path led him toward a spiritual understanding of his loss, but this is not the only way to find meaning. The critical change that happened for him was that he was willing to tell his story and then find some sense or meaning in the events. In working through your memories of loss, your goal is first and foremost to build a structure of meaning that works for you. For some people organized religion or belief in a higher power provides that structure, but for others simply a commitment to some positive legacy or greater good in their immediate relationships or community answers the problem of meaning and purpose without recourse to a higher being.

How do you get started in this building process? Like Roberto, you will need to take a series of actions that are designed to break the cycle of repetitive and paralyzing recollections. It is critical to emphasize that these steps are particularly directed to individuals who feel that their memories of loss are overwhelming them and not subsiding, despite their wish to gain greater control over their power. Importantly, most contemporary grief experts do not like to set time frames on what is considered an appropriate period of grieving. Each loss is unique and each person's response cannot be located along an expected timeline of "recovery."

Step 1: Checking with People You Trust

This step means going to your spouse, parent, sibling, close friend, pastor, or mental health professional. Ask them what they have noticed about you. Do they see you as caught up in your grief to the detriment of other aspects of your life? Do they feel that you do not show the same enjoyment or spark that they are used to seeing in you? Have they noticed any difficulties in your ability to keep up at work or with household affairs? These kinds of conversations are invaluable reality checks on how much your sorrow may have subtly taken over or altered your life, even though you may feel as if you are more or less back to normal and have kept your grief from affecting others.

Step 2: Memory Management

This step means controlling the intensity of your grief and its out-pouring. It should not be confused with denying yourself the right to grieve or to continue to experience sadness. However, the goal of this step is to give you more control over your memories' effects on your emotions and to forestall their disruption of your daily activities.

Using your memory journal, try to write down four to six memories that have come back to you repeatedly and led to bouts of strong sadness. Try to put the memories in order from most to least difficult. Now think of the same number of memories about positive events in your life that are not related to the person you have lost. These memories should be unabashedly happy ones and they should also be vivid and easy to imagine.

Once you have your two lists in place, you need to follow the relaxation training instructions as provided in exercise 6. When you have practiced your relaxation training enough to feel that you can achieve a steady, calm state, you will be ready to work on taking away some of the emotional power of your loss memories. Starting with the loss memory that is the least difficult, force yourself to think about it while in your relaxed state. As you see the images and events from that memory, you may notice yourself getting more anxious or upset. Once you detect any change in this direction, switch to your thoughts of your happier memory and concentrate on this memory until you feel yourself regaining a more relaxed state.

You will need to continue to practice this imagery work until you can allow yourself to imagine the least difficult loss memory in its totality without losing your overall state of calm. Once you have accomplished this feat, you can work yourself slowly up the ladder to each more difficult memory.

The more practice you do with relaxation and positive imagery, the faster you will be able to move up the ladder of your loss memories and the more relief you will achieve.

As you work on learning to gain more control over your feelings in response to these difficult memories, you may also need some more immediate remedies to stop your thoughts going toward these memories during the course of your day. In situations where it would be very awkward or inappropriate for you to become overwhelmed by your memories, you can use the same strategy that Roberto employed to stop his thoughts.

First, come up with a few positive affirmations to recite silently to yourself. Here are some phrases my clients have used over the years:

I can get through this.

This too shall pass.

There will be time later.

I can handle this.

Second, develop a thought-stopping technique that signals to you that you are starting to go in a direction that will disrupt your focus on the here and now. Roberto used the don't-go-there rubber band technique, but you can also just gently pinch your skin or carry a marble or smooth stone in your pocket. When the thought comes up, immediately reach for the rubber band, give yourself a gentle pinch, or feel for the stone or marble in your pocket. Once you have taken this action, it should serve as a prompt to recite your affirmation. Between the thought-stopping action and the affirmation, you should be able to redirect your focus back to the moment and away from lingering on the painful images of your memory.

Step 3: Making Meaning Out of Your Loss

As Roberto worked on reducing the disruptive effects of grief on his life, he also actively began the process of looking for something of meaning and value he could find in his loss that would take him beyond the raw hurt. For you to do this as well, the key step is to develop a sense of where this loss fits into the larger story of your life. By talking and writing about the positive lessons that you learned from this person, you are actively building an ongoing bond between the two of you. By turning your loss into a way of growing, you are doing honor to the memory of the departed person.

You can find a good concrete example of this on a Web site called Grief Steps (www.griefsteps.com), developed by Brook Noel and Pamela D. Blair, Ph.D. In an exercise on the website, they encourage you to write down affirming messages that your departed loved one has left behind with you. Your goal is to make these inspirational messages an ongoing part of your own life.

You might also try to write down a set of memories about the person in your memory journal. After each memory, try to complete the following phrase:

The positive lesson this memory has taught me is . . . .

Other acts of writing can also help. Writing a memoir, poem, or song are all ways to connect your life story to the departed person and to find meaning in both their life and their death.

The goal of each of these exercises, as the psychologist James Pennebaker (1995) has emphasized, is to take a traumatic loss, which can fragment and disrupt your sense of self, and reintegrate that painful experience into a meaningful and ultimately positive view of your life. Storytelling and the search for constructive lessons are two powerful interventions that can help you accomplish this important step in healing.

Step 4: Preserving the Person in Your Life

It is comforting to hold on to an ongoing presence of the departed person through tangible reminders of their life. Keeping the loved one's name alive through bestowing the name on children and grandchildren as a first or middle name is a highly moving and enduring way to sustain the person's legacy. Contributions to charities that will display the person's name are also an effective intervention, if you have the monetary means to pursue this avenue.

At a more symbolic level, try to imagine what the person might say in a particular situation. You might even imagine a conversation between the two of you, and what kind of advice or counsel the person might have offered.

With regard to memory, you might sometimes treat yourself to a "virtual rendez-vous" at places that you enjoyed with the departed person. Go physically to each place and then imagine your loved one's presence in that location. Give yourself the opportunity to reminisce and smile about your interactions together at that spot. Remind yourself that you can always go back to that place and recover the memories of your time together.

The point of all these preservation strategies, and any others that you might generate, is not to hide from the fact of your loss, but to acknowledge that this person continues to matter and live on as a loving presence in your life.

Step 5: Keeping Contact with the Image of Your Loved One

Keeping photographs around to look at is the obvious step here, but there are some other important ways to keep the loved one's image vibrant. Place an object that you associate with the departed person in a location that you can reach during the course of the day. It could be a shell, paperweight, brooch, watch, or book. Whatever you choose, it should be something tangible that you can see and hold; it should allow you to feel connected to something that was touched and loved by the person in their lifetime.

Step 6: Embracing the Values and Causes of Your Loved One

Perhaps the most enduring connection that you can make to the person whom you have lost is to take action that perpetuates the moral and social commitments that the two of you shared together. Whether it might be partaking in a walkathon to raise money for breast cancer research, participating in a petition drive to protect the environment, speaking up about funding for education, or marching in an ethnic pride parade, these concrete actions are statements about the passion and legacy of the departed person. In making this commitment to action, you are likely to recall moments of past action together while you are simultaneously creating new memories. In time, your children or younger people that you know may follow your example, continuing a bond that is carried forward from memory to present to future.

CONCLUDING THOUGHTS

Nothing makes a loss go away. Loss changes you and you are never the same again. Nothing can take away the inevitable ache that the finality of death brings. No one can say how long it will take your grief to lessen or how much time is too much. Yet even as you struggle with loss, it can also bring growth to your life. It can indeed make you a better person. It can make you wiser in how you choose to use your hours on this earth and in how you choose to show and accept love in your life. From memories of loss can spring greater meaning. Your life will bear on its pages the inevitable marks of sorrow that make it not a fairy tale but a truly human story.

6

Memories for Pleasure, Creativity, and Intimacy

As I write this chapter, I can see outside my study window the beginning of a winter storm. As a father and busy professional, my first reaction to this growing swirl of snowflakes is to think about the potential logistical problems they will cause. Will my daughters' school close early? What will the roads for tomorrow's commute be like?

Suddenly, I find a different scene unfolding before my mind's eye. I see myself at age eleven with my red plastic toboggan, a stopwatch, pen and paper in my hand. I am standing next to the rock garden on the snow-covered hill of my childhood home. I am in a thick wool winter coat, snow pants, and black rubber snow boots (the ones with the metal clamps that snap tight around my ankles and the red dots on the soles). The hill slopes along the side of my house, descending to a second, smaller hill that leads past a maple tree to the street below. From the rock garden to the street is no more than fifteen yards, but if I angle the toboggan run so that it traverses the second hill laterally to an apple tree, which marks the border to my neighbor's house, I can almost double the distance.

I use the stopwatch and increasingly sodden piece of paper to record the times of the various Olympic teams from France, Germany, Canada, Norway, the USA, and the dreaded USSR, which each take multiple runs down the path grooved by the plastic sled. Each team's run receives a detailed analysis by knowledgeable television commentators who evaluate the team's strengths and weaknesses. Needless to say, all of the teams, as well as the commentator roles, are ably manned by me, and in the end, the valiant team from the USA makes an unexpected comeback to snatch victory from the USSR's virtually certain grasp. The gold medal is celebrated in an indoor ceremony that features tomato soup, grilled cheese sandwiches, and hot chocolate.

Whatever hassles this current day's storm may bring, I have allowed myself for just a moment the exquisite pleasure of returning to those Olympic memories. This chapter is about enhancing your ability to achieve exactly this type of gratification—how to use your memory as a ready source of amusement and pleasure. I provide examples and strategies for getting the most enjoyment possible out of your personal memories. I also illustrate how you can recruit memories and imagery to assist in creative arts and problem solving. Finally, I discuss how couples can take advantage of shared positive memories to enhance intimacy in their relationship.

Memory is the most powerful entertainment center, creative inspiration, and aid to intimacy that you could possibly hope to find, and the best part of all is that it is absolutely free and private. When you draw on your own memory, you need not worry about subscriber costs, upgrades of equipment, or privacy violations by spam and other Internet intruders!

TURNING ON THE DVD IN YOUR BRAIN

When I teach about memories or dreams in my college classes, I often ask students if they have vivid memories and dreams. Invariably, there are several students who claim that they never dream and that their memories are virtually blank. When I ask them more about their memories, they tell me that they can remember basic incidents or facts, but all the images of the events are blurry or rather nondescript. I then explain that although some people are gifted with nearly photographic memories, most of us need to practice strategies to enhance the power and vividness of our memories (this need for practice is absolutely true for dream recall as well).

As discussed in chapter 1 of this book (see also Conway, Singer, and Tagini 2004), our memory is set up to forget as much as it is to remember. In order to be able to focus on current goals and to block irrelevant distractions from past experiences, we let go of previous events and allow their physical and emotional power to fade. At the same time that our memory is letting go of numerous images, we are also zeroing in on selected memories that connect to our current concerns. In this perpetual flux, it is easy to lose track of many memories and to struggle to recover their detail and rich physical imagery.

So to enhance my students' abilities to find the rich sensory details of past experiences, I ask them to keep the memory equivalent of a dream diary. For two straight weeks I ask them to look for one important memory each day that dates back from at least five years ago. They need to take the time to try to visualize all aspects of this memory and to experience the feelings associated with it. Once they have a clear memory in mind, they are to describe the memory in their memory journal. After repeating this exercise for two weeks, students who claimed they had virtually no sharp memories from their past report a marked change in the imagery and visual quality of their memories. They have turned on the DVD in their brain and allowed themselves to experience its sensual power. As they see each memory with enhanced clarity, they also find that many more memories are available to them than they had previously imagined. Not only has their mental reception evolved from a fuzzy black-and-white image to a high-definition flat screen TV, but they have moved from a few network channels to the wide sweep of digital cable with an almost infinite number of memory options available.

Since much of this chapter draws on your capacity to conjure up lifelike and emotionally engaging memories in your own head, it would be valuable to describe more systematically the memory recording exercise I just described. To complete this exercise, you will need both some quiet space and your memory journal.

EXERCISE 11:
FIRING UP YOUR MEMORY DVD PLAYER

1. To be successful in this memory retrieval work, you will need to set aside a little bit of time each day for fourteen days to write down a positive pleasurable memory from your life.

2. To accomplish this goal, you will need three things:

a. Your memory journal as a place to record your memories

b. A memory recording time set aside each day (right before you go to bed often works best)

c. A physical setting of peace and quiet to recall and write down your memory

3. On day 1 when you're ready to begin, you should be seated in your safe, quiet place and have your journal handy. You should not write down anything at this point.

4. Begin by asking yourself these questions: What have been some of the best times or periods in my life? Which part of my past is likely to have a number of strong positive memories in it?

5. Once you have a particular time in your life in mind, then ask yourself: Is there one particular episode, event, or moment from that time that I can recall specifically? (In the early days of this exercise, do not worry if the event or moment you select does not seem immediately vivid.)

6. Once you have selected the positive episode, event, or moment, try to answer the following initial questions:

a. What do you see in your memory? Where are you? Are you inside or outside? What do your surroundings look like? What colors, if any, do you see in the memory?

b. What sounds are there in the memory? Is there music, machinery, birdsong, or the clatter of dishes? Are there voices, radio and television sounds, car engines, or pounding waves?

c. What smells do you detect in the memory? Is there your mother's perfume, the smell of a fresh-cut lawn, or the new car scent of a just-purchased automobile? Are there hints of fudge brownies, your grandfather's aftershave, or the chicken *mole* sauce that your *abuela* prepared?

d. What tastes might you recover as you go back to that moment? Is there the sour pucker of lemonade or the syrupy sweetness of a cherry ice? Are there turkey carvings and gravy, barbequed chicken wings, or ketchup-coated French fries?

e. What sensations of touch emerge from your memory? Is there the softness of your baby's silky head, the warm water of a heated pool, or the fine oak grain of your breakfast table? Do you feel the vibrating engine of your favorite car, the immense and comforting grip of your father's hand, or the warm embrace of your college lover?

By systematically checking in with all five senses, you are helping your mind and body reacquaint itself with the physical experience of the event that may be stored more abstractly in your brain. The more physical the memory becomes, the more you can inhabit it as a living entity and enter its reality as you leave the present moment.

7. Now that you have enhanced your physical picture of your memory, you are ready to begin to move around inside it. What I mean by this is that you can begin to explore the action and activities of the events in the memory. To begin this exploration, ask yourself the following questions:

a. Who is in the memory with me? Am I alone or am I sharing this experience with family (parents, siblings, spouse, partner, children, extended family), friends, coworkers?

b. What exactly am I doing in the memory? Am I playing a sport or an instrument, acting a role in a play? Am I eating at a favorite restaurant, attending a concert, out on a date, or hiking in the woods?

c. What about the memory is making me happy? Am I enjoying the speed of motion, the touch of a loved one, or the warm glow of a glass of wine?

8. Once you have worked your way through all these questions, the memory should be much more tangible, specific, and clear to you. Now that you have it firmly in mind, take as much time as you want to savor it and live inside it.

    So often in life various people have scolded you about daydreaming or living in the past or being too nostalgic. This is your opportunity to reject all of these negatives and indulge yourself in the pure pleasure of your mind's projection screen. For this brief period, you don't have to live in the moment or move on; you can live in the luxuriant past and wallow in the sensual pleasure it has to offer you.

9. For your final step, take a few moments to write down your memory. The process of writing it down forces you to visualize the memory again as you seek to set down its specific details. It reinforces the permanence of the memory by fixing it in your brain through language as well as imagery.

    Some of you who like to write may find this part of the exercise particularly enjoyable. Others may be less inclined toward this form of expression and should not strain to write a detailed description. The major point is to have a record of the memory and to allow this record to assist you in recovering the memory whenever you would like to return to it.

10. Repeat this exercise each day. As you become more familiar with re-creating your memories, you may find that you do not need to move systematically through these questions. You will be able simply to enter each new memory and experience it visually and aurally, as well as through smell, taste, and touch. You will also be able to key in immediately on the activities and aspects of the memory that give you the most pleasure.

I should note that while you may vary how you find and enter your memory, it is critical that you keep your routine and stick with it. Training your mind to express the full power of memory is no different than training your body to run long distances or your fingers to play difficult pieces on the piano. Once you have repeated the process of searching for, settling on, and visualizing important positive memories for two weeks, you will find that the retrieval of vivid positive memories will come much more easily and proceed almost automatically.

With your enhanced memory re-creation skill, you have added an incredible resource for pleasure in your life. You can now allow your mind to return to some of your favorite memories while you do rote tasks, such as driving to work. Just for a change of pace, turn off the radio and return to a memory of a favorite moment from college days. Relive each detail and see the faces and hear the voices of your roommates again. Don't be embarrassed if you hear yourself letting out a laugh or repeating a favorite catchphrase that you all shared. Before you know it, your drive will be over and you will be pulling into the parking space at work.

Once again, some people might fear that you have done nothing productive on the drive or that you have tuned out the present. In response to these attitudes, consider the following: You have taken back control of your own mind and how you choose to amuse yourself. Instead of having your entertainment dictated to you by popular media, you have selected and created your own amusement. Further, the act of re-creating a memory involves a positive engagement of multiple areas of your brain—the visual cortex, occipital lobe, limbic system, and prefrontal cortex are all activated by the memory images. By generating powerful imagery from memory, you are exercising your brain. This activity demands more "mental muscle" than a more passive listening mode would require. In this sense, you are taking steps to protect and enhance the health of your brain, not "wasting" your mind on thoughts of days gone by.

At the same time that you are taking pleasure in your reminiscences, you are also partaking in an act of self-understanding. By re-creating the experiences that bring sustained pleasure to your life, you are identifying the activities that you find most gratifying. The very act of thinking about these experiences begs the question of how you might make more time for these activities or ones similar to them in your life. Much of this book has been about the power that memory has to motivate and guide your present actions and future plans. Memories of pleasure are no different in this regard.

Still, the fundamental point is not that these memories of pleasure have to be justified. The benefits that I have just elaborated are indeed real, but they ultimately are by-products of the true purpose of these memories, which is simply to have fun! We do not know yet what dogs or cats are thinking as they sit quietly at night staring into the firelight. Perhaps they are just smelling the air around them or listening to the distant calls of their compatriots in the streets outside. I like to think that they are letting images of past hunting successes, fat mice, and glorious sun-soaked naps pass through their memories. If this is not true and only we humans have the capacity to draw on memory's images, then consider how privileged we are to avail ourselves of this gift. Why not use it when we can, rather than always filling our minds with the noisy world or endless lists of things to do and worries about the coming day?

As with any powerful source of pleasure, moderation is key. It would not be wise to drift into a lengthy reverie of memory during an important meeting at work. Nor would it be wise to live only in these memories and seek out no new experiences. If you claim that nothing is as good or well-done as it once was, if you insist that all that came before is positive and all that we have now is inferior, you will indeed have lost the crucial balance between old and new that allows you to gain the greatest benefit from memory.

However, with balance, a world of memory's pleasures awaits you. As you drive to work, listen to quiet music at night, or sit with your coffee in the morning, you can in a moment's notice engage the DVD inside your head and take in a world of rich vibrant imagery and sensual delight.

MEMORIES AS A SOURCE OF CREATIVITY

The great novelist and essayist Vladimir Nabokov once wrote about the potential expanse of memory:

> How small the cosmos (a kangaroo's pouch would hold it),
> how paltry and puny in comparison to human consciousness,
> to a single individual recollection, and its expression in
> words. (Nabokov 1966, 24)

Later in this same passage, he talks about seeing blinking lights from a hillside while traveling on a train as a child. Their beauty was like diamonds on black velvet, and the richness of this memory was so vast, that he later "gave [it] away to my characters to relieve the burden of my wealth" (p. 24).

Fiction and poetry, not to mention visual art and music, build on memory. Eugene O'Neill described himself as writing *Long Day's Journey into Night*, a thinly disguised autobiographical play, through a constant filter of recollection and tears. Khaled Hosseini, author of *The Kite Runner*, a recent best seller about an Afghan boy's betrayal of his close friend, drew on his own boyhood in Kabul in order to paint the rich portrait of social class distinctions in Afghan society.

In each of these cases, these authors do not simply plug into memory and then download their experiences onto the page. Memory is a starting point that leads to the creation of new characters and experiences that are shaped by the author's imagination. Yet writers need not be the only ones who can use their memories to take them to new uncharted regions. All of us have the capacity to tap into our memories and emerge with ideas and insights that go beyond our initial recollections. Starting with a memory, we can generate imagery and alternate endings to the events we recall. These embellishments can be used for simple amusement (just like the memory for pleasure described in the previous section), but they can also be a source of creative art and problem solving. The next exercise helps you explore how to connect your memories to different aspects of creativity.

EXERCISE 12: TAPPING THE CREATIVE POTENTIAL OF MEMORY

For this exercise you will once again need your memory journal and a quiet place that gives you a chance for some uninterrupted and reflective time. You will again retrieve important memories from your life and then write them down in your memory journal. However, this exercise is broken up into three distinct purposes:

1. Finding a memory to enhance for pleasure

2. Finding a memory for problem solving

3. Finding a memory as a source of creative art

Part 1: Memory Enhancement for Pleasure

1. Choose one of the memories that you have previously identified as a pleasurable memory.

2. Take your usual steps to re-create the memory. Once you are well immersed in the memory and enjoying its images and sensations, you can then proceed with steps to enhance it.

3. First, identify what is giving you pleasure and enjoyment. For example, imagine you are recalling a delicious Italian meal that you had at a restaurant in Little Italy in New York City. As you recall that special evening, you are picturing the red-checkered tablecloth, the free-flowing Chianti, the steaming plate of rigatoni in marinara, and the crusty warm bread with melting butter on your plate. The restaurant is dimly lit, couples are huddled at small tables, and the black-suited waiters are weaving among the tables like graceful dancers. In this stream of images, you identify the Mediterranean atmosphere, the romantic feeling, and the pleasure of your husband's company as the chief features of your delight.

4. With these features in mind, you can now let your imagination expand on them with a few creative twists. For example, if you like the Mediterranean ambiance, why not move the memory to Venice and put the dinner table on a terrace overlooking the sea? Next, imagine that your husband and you are a few years younger and a few pounds trimmer. Change your Ann Taylor dress to a Versace gown. Change his Brooks Brothers blazer to an Armani suit. Have the two of you hold hands together under the table while you add the subtle sounds of a distant street singer performing a Verdi aria. Fill up each of your glasses of wine. Linger as long as you want, and then imagine the two of you strolling back arm in arm to a sumptuous hotel suite awaiting you.

5. If you are so inclined, it can be fun to write down the enhanced memory in your memory journal. It can then be used as a favorite daydream to recruit during a dreary day

or night. You might even decide to share it with your spouse at some point as a source of amusement or inspiration.

Part 2: Enhancing Memories for Problem Solving

1. Now your goal is to recruit a memory from your life that is not simply a memory of unabashed pleasure or fun. You are looking for a memory that contains conflict, struggle, or confusion in it. It should end in ambivalence or uncertainty. The key ingredient in the memory is that it contains elements that don't fit together neatly.

    For example, a patient of mine had a memory about a work situation in which he felt his boss did not recognize his contribution to a major project. He had wanted to speak up about this slight, but somehow never found the opportunity.

    Your memory can be about a problem at work, but it could also be about an athletic challenge, an interpersonal conflict, or an economic worry.

2. Once you have the memory in mind, write down a description of it in your memory journal and then answer the following questions:

    a. How would you define the problem in your memory?

    b. What is causing the tension or conflict in the memory?

    c. What feelings do you associate with the struggle depicted in the memory?

    d. Why do you think the problem was not resolved?

3. Now that you've taken steps to define the memory's conflict, you are ready to explore creative solutions.

    a. Try to imagine alternative resolutions to the memory's dilemma. Sit for a while with each imagined ending—allow yourself to experience the feelings associated with each outcome. Does one feel more "right" or comfortable than any of the other possibilities?

For example, the patient described previously imagined sending an e-mail to his boss expressing his concern. He also imagined having a face-to-face meeting. Ultimately, he felt that it would work best to talk in person with his boss.

b. Once you have imagined an alternative ending that feels best to you, try to imagine how it might have changed subsequent experiences or interactions.

My patient created a scenario where his boss was initially surprised but then made a commitment to show more awareness of his contributions and even gave him more responsibility in the future.

c. At each point in this imagined future, try to see how it would feel and whether this fictitious future fits with your desires and wishes, as well as with what is most realistic and likely to occur. The answers to these questions are the closest you can get to a "gut check" without actually jumping in and acting on the resolution that you have imagined.

d. When the struggle in the memory involves an interpersonal conflict, there is another direction in which you can take your imagination. This technique is called *reverse role-playing*. Your job is to try to imagine that you have taken on the role of the person with whom you are having a conflict. Make a sincere effort to live inside this other person's head for a while. Try to say things and do things that would allow you to experience the world as they do. This technique can be very effective in breaking interpersonal logjams, and is one that I quite frequently use with my patients in couples therapy.

Part 3: Enhancing Memories for Creativity

1. For those of you who are inclined toward different forms of creative expression, these same exercises can be inspiring starting points for artistic efforts. Once again, time set aside, a quiet place, and your memory journal are the key ingredients for getting started on this process.

2. Try several days of keeping your memory journal, writing memories down that have a particularly strong emotional impact for you, whether positive or negative.

3. Choose one memory that has a particularly vivid image or unusual twist associated with its story. Once you have settled on the memory, try to imagine it not as your own memory, but happening to another person.

4. Now tell the story of the incident happening to this person. Tell the story in a straightforward fashion. Once you have this bit of writing done, answer the following questions:

    a. What was this person doing before this incident occurred?

    b. What will this person do as a result of this incident?

5. Now try to describe in the same language as the original memory this imagined past event and this imagined future event. You now have three scenes that could form the nucleus of a short story.

    For example, one of my patients told me a memory from when he was ten years old and he and his friend found a bag filled with $10,000 next to a dumpster behind a restaurant. This unusual memory could be used as the hinge for a very interesting short story about how a ten-year-old child's life might be changed by such a monumental event.

6. If the memory is more a single powerful image rather than a series of events, try to think about its image as the starting point for a poem or drawing. Remember, the object is to let yourself open up to your own creative powers. You don't need to worry about showing these efforts to anyone else.

This exercise is ultimately for you to enjoy the process of freeing your imagination and allowing your memories to connect to new modes of feeling, seeing, and expressing yourself.

To help illustrate these exercises, let us take a look at a concrete example from my practice work.

Larry and the Swim Across Loon Lake—A Case Example

Larry was a patient of mine in his midfifties who worked in a machine shop. Years of heavy physical duties had impaired his mobility and left him in chronic pain. It was difficult for him to do any significant physical exercise, and on most days he was grateful to go home and simply work his way into a warm bath. He had tried many different pain treatment programs and physical therapies, but had reconciled himself to a life of restricted movement and limited physical activity. Although he had not given up on improving his physical condition, he asked me to help lift his current mood and outlook.

We agreed to work on a memory exercise that he could use for amusement and stress relief. When he described the brief release that he felt as he eased into his warm bath at the end of the day, I asked him about any positive memories associated with water he might have. He described to me a memory of camping as a teen when he had tented next to Loon Lake in Oregon. One morning he had swum far out into the lake and felt like he could swim forever without tiring.

We used this memory as our starting point, and I took him through all the steps of imagining the sights, sounds, and feelings of the memory. We then worked on enhancing the memory. He imagined swimming across the lake, standing on the opposite shore, lying on a sunny beach, then jumping back in and swimming with powerful pain-free strokes. As Larry grew more adept at using imagery, he found this memory a terrific source of pleasure and comfort. It became part of his evening ritual that he would allow himself a few minutes of "memory swimming" at Loon Lake during his evening bath. Interestingly, he told me that he often found that he needed less pain treatment after a really enjoyable period of imagery.

MEMORY AS AN AID IN INTIMACY

Thus far, I have provided concrete methods for you to put your memories to work as sources of amusement, problem solving, and creativity. In this final section of this chapter, let us look at how couples can employ shared memories as aids in building intimacy and erotic pleasure.

As a therapist who sees a large number of couples in therapy, I am well aware of the struggles couples with children have in maintaining the intimate romantic aspects of their partnership. Each day is a campaign that starts with racing to get to work while helping the children prepare for school. Each evening begins in an already exhausted state with a night of dishes, laundry, lunch making, bill paying, story reading, and virtual collapse into bed already assured. In the midst of this, it is very difficult to find the time or the spirit to give romantically to each other.

I work with couples intensively to restructure their time and to carve out moments for intimacy and "date nights" that honor the importance of the couple as a couple. No matter how much I emphasize the importance of creating these opportunities, it is an ongoing struggle for many couples.

Here is where memory can come in. Sitting across from a depleted and frayed couple, I ask them if there was ever a time when they experienced a wonderful romantic connection. Without fail, they nod enthusiastically and can quickly agree on an earlier period (usually before children) when there was quite a bit of ardor and romantic heat. I then ask the couple to identify a specific day or night that they can recall and agree on as being one of their peak moments of romance. After a bit of self-consciousness and blushing, they usually come up with a vivid and lovely moment of connection. Once they have identified this memory, I then give them the following instructions to follow as a homework assignment to enhance intimacy in their relationship.

EXERCISE 13: INTIMATE MEMORIES— "BACK TO THE FUTURE"

1. Once you have settled on the memory that you will use, you need to pick a night three or four days later that will be your "Back to the Future" night. Let's say that you have chosen the memory on a Monday, then you might select Thursday night to be the night to do the exercise.

2. With the night chosen, you have three days to build up the anticipation and excitement about this "romantic trip" you are about to take. To allow the momentum to build, each of you should make a brief call to the other mentioning the upcoming night. You should send each

other a teasing e-mail or leave a note at the breakfast table or on a pillow.

3. If you have pictures from the time period of the memory, you might want to take a glance at them when you have a chance or include them with a note for your partner.

4. As the night approaches, make sure that you have planned out the household duties of the evening to allow you to have them under control and the two of you in bed at a reasonable hour. The key to making this happen and not having your plans sabotaged is to accept that not everything on the household list has to be completed nor perfectly in place. For one night you are going to make the two of you a more important priority than the rest of the household concerns.

    If for any reason an emergency occurs (such as a child gets sick, a crisis arises at work, the hot water heater bursts), you must commit to an alternate date and again set that date in stone.

5. Once you two have settled into the bed and closed off any other possible distractions, you are ready to begin your journey back in time. In order to allow the images of the past to rise up in your imagination, it is best to lie together in darkness or else in very soft candlelight.

6. Ideally, as you describe the memory out loud, each of you takes a turn describing the physical details of the setting, how you each looked, the sounds, smells, tastes, and so on. To trade off, one person can describe a scene or situation and then ask, "Would you like to tell the next part?"

    However, it is also perfectly all right if you prefer to have one be more of the narrator and the other a very receptive listener. Whoever is doing the narrating should strive to emphasize the sensual details of the memory. Paint a picture of the romantic setting, whether palm trees or hotel suite or cozy farmhouse. Describe the soft music, the lapping waves, or the crackling fire, and then move on to how each of you looked—thick shining hair, tanned bodies, smells of perfume or cologne, gorgeous eyes, or sexy smiles.

One rule that you should have as you continue to build the romance of the memory is that you can touch and stroke each other as you tell the memory out loud, but you cannot engage in any sustained kissing or more intense contact until you have allowed yourselves to explore and return to the memory in some detail. Using the enhancement techniques described above, you may also decide to embellish the memory and give it even more sensual or romantic details as you both share the description of it with each other.

7. When it is clear that both of you have truly lost yourselves in the memory and given in to its excitement and passion, you can then let go and use the present moment to create an experience that you will also want to remember.

This is why the exercise is called "Back to the Future"—its goal is to use the past to create an exciting and intimate future for you both.

Will and Liza—A Case Example

Will and Liza, a couple in their late thirties, came to see me for couples therapy and assured me that things were pretty much hopeless between them. They felt more like roommates or business partners than husband and wife. They were running their household as best they could, paying the bills, taking care of the kids (three children all under ten), and doing their best to get to church each Sunday. Will kept fit by going for runs a few times a week, and Liza was involved in a yoga class. I could not even keep track of the number of after-school activities the children pursued. One or another child was always needing a ride to scout meetings, soccer practice, dance rehearsal, youth chorus, or math explorers.

Then there were doctors, dentists, optometrists, and dermatologists. Will's work required him to travel to a satellite office twice a week, meaning he had to leave extra early (5:30 A.M.) and could not be home before 7:30 P.M. on those days. Liza was required to work at least twenty hours if she wanted to keep her health benefits. They tried their best for family dinners, but sports practices, recitals, late nights at work, and church committee meetings increasingly made these communal meals a challenge. Ten-year-old Wyatt and six-year-old Mary were safely asleep by 8:30, but Elsa, the one-and-a-half-year-old, known as the "Energizer Bunny" by the rest of the family, was a different story. Multiple bedtime stories, backrubs, and, ultimately, Will lying next to her, might get her to bed by 9:30 on a good night.

After these marathon evenings, Liza would have to rouse Will from his slumber next to Elsa and lead him half asleep to their own bedroom. If she succeeded in waking him, they might meet for a brief to-do list summit in the kitchen before giving in to utter fatigue. Regarding their marriage, it felt lifeless and increasingly loveless. They did not want to divorce—it was almost like they did not have time or energy for that—but they also did not want to go on in this zombielike existence of routine and numbness. So what could they do?

I started by asking them to ponder more seriously the question of staying together. In fact, my first homework assignment was for them each to take a quiet period of reflection separately in the coming week. They should each ask themselves, "Do I still love my partner? Do I still have hope that this marriage could improve and return to a more active intimate relationship?" Based on their answers to these questions, we would set our goal for couples therapy accordingly.

Though couples with whom I work come back with all different variations of answers to these fundamental questions, Will and Liza were united in their belief that they still loved each other and wanted to see the marriage improve. Unfortunately, they were also united in the view that nothing could change until the children were much older, and this might be too late for any prospects of rekindling romance between them.

Once I had the first part of their reply—a continued expression of love for each other despite the gathering distance and alienation—there was little doubt in my mind that their lives could be improved dramatically without the need for dissolving the relationship. As a therapist, I cannot cause love to emerge when it is no longer felt or was not there in the first place, but I certainly can help stoke the power of love that continues to be present, no matter how dormant it has become.

In trying to revive more romantic intimacy with a couple, it is critical to know what their frequency of intimacy at its peak was (usually in the first months or early years of their relationship). Over time I have learned that there is wide variation in the frequency and intensity of intimate contact. Some couples, for whatever reasons, seldom made love more than once every couple of weeks, even during the early years of their marriage.

Will and Liza had had a strong intimate connection and still claimed to feel attraction to each other (at least in theory—there was little recent practice to bear out this claim). They described a vacation weekend the previous summer where they had been able to find time for intimacy and how much they had still enjoyed each other. The fall and winter, however, had been a time of drifting apart and increasing tension about their lack of intimacy. Rather than fight or feel frustrated, they had virtually given up trying.

Once again, this information gave me a great deal of optimism. It was clear that under the right circumstances they were a good romantic match and could find excitement and pleasure with each other. So with some skepticism and anxiety on their part, we agreed that we would work on methods to build more intimacy and romance back into their relationship.

As we have previously acknowledged, time is the great thief of romance from couples' lives, so the place to start was to make them commit to giving this aspect of their marriage a renewed sense of priority. I worked with Will and Liza on this exact calendar challenge over several sessions, which involved bringing in mutual schedules, exploring the possibilities of how relatives and babysitters could give them breaks from the children, and planning date nights and time together. I also made them confront ways in which they might actually avoid each other out of fear of expectations or simple fatigue.

These efforts brought some successes, but also highlighted the inescapable whirlwind of contemporary life for a household of two working parents and three active children. So as we worked on carving out time, I proposed the "Back to the Future" exercise as an opportunity to build up intimacy without requiring new activities or time away from home. It was certainly not a substitute for the efforts to restructure their lives, but it could serve as a valuable spur to remind them of how good life could be if they made the effort to build romance into their lives again.

Will and Liza agreed to try out the exercise and selected a memory of a ski trip to a bed-and-breakfast in Vermont that they had taken before their children were born. They recalled long days of skiing in ideal conditions and then delicious meals with good red wine in front of fires smelling of pinewood and hickory. Despite the exertion of the day, they still had enough energy for passionate lovemaking before settling into deep contented sleep.

They agreed this was a high-point memory that they could use, and they set a date four nights later to practice the full routine of the exercise. As might be expected, Elsa developed an ear infection, Wyatt's model of a pyramid started to become unglued, and Will's boss needed him to spend an extra day at the satellite office. They came back to our next session not only having failed to do the exercise, but feeling more disheartened than at any point in our work.

My only two interventions were to make them confirm to each other that they really wanted to achieve the goal we had agreed on—to find their way back to some romance in their relationship—and to make them commit to setting up a new night. I told them that it was not uncommon for the first attempt to go down in flames. Besides the fact that their lives were indeed very busy, there was the fact that they were both scared to death of the promise that they were making. There was a part of them that wanted nothing more than to escape the risk of opening up again and feeling all the intensity that intimacy demanded. Better to watch a *CSI* episode, surf the Net, or simply go to sleep. If they came back to me again saying it did not work, I would agree that things were impossible and we could all give up. The part of them that wanted the safe routine would have won, and they could then continue along their unthreatening but passion-numbing path. I concluded by saying that the problem with this line of thought was that they had asked me to achieve a goal with them that was the opposite of their familiar routine, and that they had committed to each other to reach this goal. So they better try again.

Still skeptical, but recognizing the importance of following through on their commitment, they set up the next "Back to the Future" ski trip. We reviewed all the steps they should take building up to the night—phone calls, e-mails, notes, pictures—and I also made them promise to have no intimate contact before that night (a promise they thought they would be very unlikely to break). The next session Will and Liza came into the meeting, sat down, and looked at me with embarrassed smiles. They had indeed completed their homework assignment with flying colors, and asked me if it would be okay to plan another memory trip very soon. Most importantly, within a few more weeks, they had put the wheels in motion to go on an actual weekend together, with grandparents filling in to watch the children while they were away. Life continued to be chaotic, but at least now they were learning how to give their own intimacy and romance a place amidst that chaos.

CONCLUDING THOUGHTS

The message of this chapter is simple. Your memory does not exist only to remind you where you put your keys the night before or to prompt you to pick up your daughter from day care. Your memory should not remind you only of embarrassing moments, mistakes you've made, and losses in your life. Your memory is there to be an island of pleasure and a threshold to an illimitable land of imagination.

It holds images and stories to be summoned and enhanced by your mind's eyes and ears and other senses. Far from being a stagnant pool where you wallow in nostalgia and block out the present, your memory can be a rushing torrent of possibility—a chief tributary to the stream of consciousness, filling it with episodes of delight, excitement, and triumph that you have lived before and can now revive. Ultimately, the key to getting the most pleasure out of your memory is to see your memory not as time frozen in the past, but as part of your present and future. The past is still alive, still seeks to be vibrant in your thoughts, and when you actively engage your memory with emotion and creativity, it does indeed live again and grow, and so do you.

7

Memories and Memory-Telling from Birth to Death

My fifteen-year-old daughter Olivia's earliest memory is of seeing a black snake lying on a rock near a stream while we were walking home from the local breakfast place in town. I remember that day and would estimate that she was no more than two and a half years old on that walk. Why of all the thousands of memories from that period of her life has that one stuck with her? It is hard to say. It might be because of the oddity of the moment—seeing something slightly threatening on our ritual Sunday walk for chocolate milk and donuts, or maybe because it was a piece of important news that she could put into words and tell her mother when we returned to the house, or maybe because it was something that we could always share in the future ("Remember that walk to town when we saw the black snake on the rock?"). What has become clear over the years is that this memory shares a double function—it is both a memory that belongs to her and a memory that belongs to us, her family.

This chapter helps you to explore the role of memory across your entire life span, starting literally from before you were born and extending to the legacy of your memories after you have departed this world. Its key theme is that our memories are never just our own. As children we learn ways of remembering from our parents; in adolescence we organize our memories into life stories based on cultural roles provided to us; in young adulthood we strive to coordinate and blend our story with the story of a life partner; by middle adulthood we become increasingly concerned with the impact our story is having on others (including our own offspring); and by late adulthood we are asking who will preserve our story, who will continue to tell our memories, and will we even be remembered at all?

At each of these five phases of life, there are concrete steps that you can take to build stronger memories and stronger connections to the people who help you to shape your memories. As you can see, this is a chapter as much about what the memory researcher Avril Thorne (2000) calls "memory-telling" as it is about the memories themselves. Let us begin at the beginning with how your memories are shaped before your birth and then move through each of the phases of life until we finish with the legacy of your memory in your last years.

BIRTH STORIES

Do you know the story of your own birth? Do you know where your mother was when she went into labor? Do you know what time of day it was? Do you know what your father was doing at the time? Was he standing by with a stopwatch, timing contractions? Did he leave work and rush to the hospital? Do you know how long the labor lasted or how loud you cried once you were delivered?

In a study of the transmission of these birth stories from mothers to daughters and how these stories can reflect strong ties between the two, my colleagues and I asked approximately sixty college-aged women to tell us their birth stories (Hayden, Singer, and Chrisler 2004). We asked them who had told them the story and how often they had heard the story. We also asked them to rate the strength of their bond to their mother and their own sense of self-esteem. Then we asked them to contact their mothers and get them to write down their own versions of their daughters' births. More than thirty mothers agreed to e-mail or post us their stories.

Once we had all the stories in hand, we studied the stories for content. What were the most common incidents? How much did the stories emphasize the difficulty of giving birth or the joy of their daughter's arrival? Perhaps of greatest interest, we wondered how close a match there might be between the mothers' and daughters' stories. We asked three raters to see how successfully they could match the correct stories with each other.

What did we learn? First, all daughters but one in our study had heard their birth stories from their mothers. So these memories do indeed reflect a shared mother-daughter experience. On average, the daughters had heard the story at least twice from their mothers. The daughters' stories of their birth focused primarily on details about the hospital, delivery, and their arrival, along with some information about their father, siblings, and relatives. Although the mothers' recollections included these same details, their stories also shared much more information about their prehospital preparation and their personal feelings during the whole experience. Here is an example of one of the more detailed birth stories we collected from the daughters:

> My parents were twenty-five years old and they had been
> married about a year when my mom found out she was
> pregnant. She was incredibly happy, as was my father. I was
> born two weeks late. My mom went into labor during the
> night, but it wasn't overly painful, so she decided to wait a
> while to go to the hospital. My mom remembers eating a ton
> of cherry Jell-O, and taking a shower, counting the roses on
> the wallpaper. She still didn't want to leave, but my dad
> convinced her. All in all, it wasn't overly painful. Supposedly,
> I was crying before I was born. I had Apgars of 10 and 10,
> which my mother is very proud of, because she had no drugs
> during labor, just a lot of yoga. They called my grandparents
> who (as they tell me on my birthday every year) jumped in
> the car. My aunt, a nurse at another hospital, kept her uni-
> form on and snuck into the nursery to find me. I had crazy
> black hair and was seven pounds, ten ounces, and twenty-one
> and a half inches long. My mom tells me this story in great
> detail every year on my birthday.

How might the ability to recount such a vivid and detailed story about your birth reflect something about your relationship with your mother or your own self-esteem? We rated each story for its level of descriptiveness, as well as its overall degree of positive emotion. We then correlated the strength of the mother-daughter bond and the daughters' self-esteem (as measured by our self-report scales) with our ratings of the descriptiveness and positive emotion of the daughters' birth stories. Daughters who felt closer and more able to confide in their mothers wrote stories that were more descriptive, while indicating they had heard the stories from their mothers more frequently. In addition, daughters with higher self-esteem described more detailed and positive birth stories.

When we looked at the mothers' stories, we found the same strong relationships. More positive and descriptive accounts by the mothers of their daughters' births predicted daughters with higher self-esteem and stronger mother-daughter bonds. Most importantly, when our raters matched mothers' and daughters' stories, we found that more correct matches of stories were made for daughters with higher self-esteem and stronger bonds to their mothers. In other words, daughters whose memories matched their mother's memories felt better about themselves and their relationship to their mother.

Our research suggests that the story we form of our lives begins even before our own memory is capable of creating more permanent memories. Our very first moments of life are recorded in our parents' and relatives' memories, and we then rely on their testimonials to form a picture of our origins. Certainly, the facts of our birth play a role in how the story shapes up, but so also do the narrators (for example, mother, father, grandparent) who craft the story into a more permanent narrative that is shared among the family.

In this kind of study we cannot know the direction of the relationships we found. Do happy birth experiences lead to positive feelings about oneself and a strong mother-child bond? Or do self-esteem and a warm maternal relationship cause one to color the story of one's birth in the most positive of hues? Though we cannot provide definitive answers to these questions, we can see the powerful relationship between a positive account of your own origins in this world and your sense of security and comfort living in it.

EXERCISE 14:
STUDYING YOUR OWN BIRTH STORY

1. Using your memory journal, try to write down all that you know about the circumstances of your birth.

2. Now, the next step depends on whether or not you might be able to ask your mother for her account. If your mother is no longer alive or not in a state to be able to give you her version of your birth story, it is still possible that you might be able to find an account in a baby album or a diary that your mother kept.

    If you are lucky enough to be able to compare your account with your mother's, what do you notice about the overlap between the two? Are they very similar in detail and emphasis?

    Do you notice any ways in which the story may contain an image, metaphor, or theme that captures something enduring about your life or your relationship with your mother? If so, try to put this image or idea down in words.

3. Whatever you learn about your birth, try to see this information as an opening chapter to a life that is continuing to unfold. No amount of detail in your birth story can capture the mystery of that moment—what you felt as you came from darkness into light—and inevitably, all memories that follow will also contain a similar incompleteness.

PARENT-CHILD TALK: THE BEGINNINGS OF MEMORIES AS STORIES

From our birth story, the next part of our memory journey is what Robyn Fivush and Elaine Reese (2002) call "parent-child talk about the past." My Sunday walk with Olivia when she spotted the snake is a perfect example of how parents teach children how to organize their experiences into orderly, sequential narratives. We repeatedly talked about the incident immediately in the aftermath and then many times over the years. Fivush and Reese, over numerous studies, have demonstrated that parents guide very young children in how to provide the necessary details in telling a story, how to know what information to include or exclude, how to know what events should follow or precede other events, and how to give accounts of their feelings and reactions to events, along with several other important skills.

Even more, they have demonstrated that the act of reminiscing together is an important form of bonding between parent and child. It grounds both lives in a common experience and builds a tradition of these experiences that creates a deep-layered connection. This connection through shared memory helps to define what the words "relationship," "intimacy," or "family," in fact actually mean.

A key component that distinguishes children who develop stronger abilities in reminiscing is the degree to which the parents model good memory-telling by providing cues that call for elaboration of the memory by the child.

Fivush and Reese and their colleagues have conducted longitudinal studies that show that mothers' ability to ask elaborative questions of children as young as eighteen months can predict children's ability to reminisce at three or four years. Even more, parents who emphasize the emotional and interpretive aspects of the memories ("feeling" questions, "why" questions, questions about "good or bad" or "like" versus "dislike") are more likely to have children who later highlight these same aspects in their spontaneous telling of memories. These researchers have also found a connection between more elaboration in parent-child talk and more secure and stronger bonds among parents and children.

Interestingly, there also tend to be gender differences in how parents handle reminiscing with their children. Regardless of whether it is a mother or father talking to their children, parents engage in more elaboration and emotion with daughters compared to sons. This finding confirms the adult research that shows a clear advantage of women over men in generating more detailed and emotional memories. When Fivush and Reese looked at the particular emotional differences in memories discussed by parents with girls and boys, they noticed some of the biggest differences were in the greater willingness of parents to discuss sad memories with their daughters versus their sons. In contrast, their conversations with boys tended to emphasize more physical circumstances, objective events, and facts.

These results strongly suggest that how parents teach children to recall their lives is simultaneously reinforcing messages for them about their roles in society. By encouraging expressive and emotional memories, girls are learning to communicate emotions, to share experiences good and bad, and to make sense of their worlds through dialogue. In contrast, boys are learning that memory-telling is functional and directed toward the communication of facts and information. They are learning to limit the emotional content and to stick to the "objective" details ("just the facts, ma'am"). In this way their interpersonal context is more instrumental, isolated, and less expressive of shared experience. Is it any wonder that the couples I see in therapy have such difficulty in understanding what each other is saying or in agreeing on the details of past experiences that they have shared together?

EXERCISE 15: TALKING WITH YOUR CHILDREN ABOUT MEMORIES

Since the research on parent-child talk points to the strong value of questions and elaboration in helping children develop their memories, here are some hints for how you might talk with your own children to promote strong memory development.

1. Prompt the child to talk about shared experiences (for example, walks to the park, trips to the grocery store, a TV show watched together, a book read out loud, or a family picnic).

2. Ask very specific questions that stay at the level of detail that a child might notice. (What did we wear? Who was with us? What did you see there? What did we do there?)

3. If the child is unsure about a response, give prompts and hints that help them to know what details to provide. (We wore our rain boots, didn't we? You wore your red hat, and what hat did I wear? Jimmy came along, but did Sarah come too?)

4. Give strong praise for any answers and details they provide. Make sure to follow up on any spontaneous details they provide. Ask questions about these details in order to allow them to tell their own recollections as they uniquely recall them. (That's great that you remember the doggie! Tell me what color the dog was. Was he a friendly dog?)

5. Encourage the child to build sequences of events. (Then what happened? And then? And what happened after that?)

6. Ask about the child's feelings. (Did you feel happy at the park? What made you sad about the show? Were you angry at the bad man in the puppet show?)

7. Ask the child about others' feelings. (Was Jimmy happy at the park? When you got home, was Sarah sad that she did not go?)

ADOLESCENCE: THE BEGINNING OF THE LIFE STORY

Let's take our two-and-a-half-year-old Olivia who spotted the snake by the stream and fast-forward to her current age of fifteen. In recent months, this very bright and thoughtful adolescent has taken to referring to herself in the third person. She will say, "Olivia will be busy with her homework tonight and will not be emerging from her room again," or "Olivia does not find that funny." This stepping back from herself and portraying herself as a character in the ongoing saga of our family is a cardinal example of the development of self-consciousness in adolescence.

The great theorist of cognitive development, Jean Piaget, described adolescence as a time in which individuals develop a capacity for abstraction and consideration of hypothetical situations. Adolescents have acquired an ability to see multiple solutions to problems based not always in the concrete world but in their imagination. Whereas younger children tend to be bound by rules and their immediate sensory experience, adolescents begin to entertain idealistic scenarios of what might be; they question the status quo and ask why rules must be maintained or traditions observed.

At the center of this shift in thinking about the world are their shifting thoughts about themselves. They are no longer simply the son or daughter of their parents, defined by their particular family's values, rituals, opinions, or preferences. They now begin to ask themselves who they are distinct from their family's orbit. As their bodies go through the rapid and sometimes disorienting changes associated with puberty and growth into young adulthood, they can stand back from the mirror and ask, "Who indeed is this person reflecting back at me?"

Where does memory fit into this process of emerging identity? When adolescents embark on the task of self-definition, they draw on whatever pieces of data they can find to make sense of their exploration. They look desperately to peers for confirmation of their efforts to convey a sense of personal style. They look to accomplishments in athletics, schoolwork, music, dance, or community service to give them a niche in their social hierarchies and to be distinguishable from the crowd. As they work in the present to build up an external identity—a way of being noticed by the world around them—they are also wrestling with internal questions: How have I come to be the way I am? Why do I do things that I do? Will I ever reach my goals?

The answers to these questions are partly found in the previous experiences from their lives—the successes and failures, moments of family joys or sorrows—that comprise the episodes of their life stories. According to researchers Habermas and Bluck (2000), adolescents engage in the first efforts to unite the memories of their lives into a coherent story that expresses important themes and desires that become guideposts for adulthood. They launch themselves into what David Elkind (1981) called "personal fables" that collect the events of their lives into a tale of noble purpose and lofty ambition. At the center of this tale they see themselves from that third-person distance as heroes and heroines braving the challenges and pitfalls of a confusing and often alienating world.

As new events occur in adolescents' lives, they increasingly weave these events into a developing self-narrative—the life story of identity discussed in detail in chapter 3. David Rubin (Rubin, Rahhal, and Poon 1998), a researcher in autobiographical memory, has demonstrated that the memories formed in the age period of fifteen to twenty-four end up having the greatest staying power of all memories formed across the decades of the life span. He calls this special retention of memories from our adolescent years a "reminiscence bump" and has found it over multiple studies and samples.

Why do memories during adolescence endure and remain particularly vivid and powerful for adults of all ages? Perhaps the reason lies in adolescents' simultaneous efforts to begin the construction of a meaningful and coherent life story. As they begin to write their story, every first experience, athletic triumph, romantic heartbreak, or confrontation with a parent, is seared into the pages of this story, leaving an indelible impression for the years to come.

As adolescents forge their life stories, they look everywhere for reference points that will give their narrative a sense of coherence, purpose and meaning. They rely on characters from literature and film, role models of teachers and coaches, the imagined lives of celebrities and public figures, and, most of all, their parents' examples to provide them with touchstones for how to imagine themselves and their own lives. Identification with heroes, pop stars, rebels, athletes, and older youth (including siblings) can dramatically influence how they think about and craft the episodes, themes, and major characters of their own life story. Whatever we can do as parents to encourage their exposure to positive role models and uplifting activities cannot be underestimated. Adolescents' minds are laying out the fundamental narrative structure that will tend to carry them forward for their adult life that lies just ahead. Helping them align their memories and self-definition with an identity organized around positive relationships, hard-won achievements, and commitment to community and faith will have profound repercussions for the decades ahead. Parents and adults who have contact with adolescents need to do everything in their power to help them open the story of their life with chapters steeped in hope, possibility, and a sense of support for their future aspirations. The story that emerges is inevitably the unique creation and possession of the adolescent who crafts it, but it is a story that is shaped in the crucible of family, peers, community, and the myriad influences of culture.

YOUNG ADULTHOOD: THE MERGING OF LIFE STORIES

Although there are many challenges that we face in our twenties and thirties—finding a productive niche in the workforce, setting up a household separate from parents, building a sense of community and civic involvement, laying the groundwork for financial security—the concern that is most prominent for the majority of young adults is finding an intimate partner and making a long-term commitment. E. H. Erikson (1959, 1963) described the central question of this period as "intimacy versus isolation" and indeed many young adults despair over whether or not they will ever find someone to love who will love them in return.

As individuals reach a committed intimacy with another person, they face the complex task of blending the life story they have been fashioning since adolescence with this other person's intricate and multilayered story. You may share the story of your childhood with your partner, and slowly that story becomes part of their story. They may tell you about an important argument they had with their father and now you have that story inside you too. Slowly, as you accumulate memories about your own relationship, these stories become your shared property and help to define exactly what your relationship means to you both.

For example, one older couple shared this powerful romantic memory of their first period of being together. Even though they were currently struggling with each other, they could return to this memory as an embodiment of their mutual attraction. Here is the memory told by the wife:

> *He used to come by to my little apartment after he finished work. It would be fairly late. I would try to have a little pasta dinner ready and he would bring a bottle of red wine. He would still be in his suit from work and look so dashing. We would put on Frank Sinatra, open the window to let the cooler night air in, and sometimes just dance around the living room. Things would get pretty hot and heavy, if you know what I mean. I lived for those nights. I felt like we were a couple they ought to make a movie about. He made me feel like all the adventure and romance I could ever want was in that room. He made me feel anything was possible.*

The husband's shared pleasure in this memory confirmed what a central place it occupied not simply in either of their psyches, but in the mutual world their relationship had created. As younger couples work to build sustained committed relationships, they are constantly feeling out their ability to create these shared memories that express the best elements of their slowly intermingling stories.

One obstacle to this successful blending can be the rigidity or already determined nature of their stories about relationships. In earlier chapters, we have talked about the idea of "scripts" in personality— those cookie-cutter sequences of events and emotions that we carry inside us and tend to impose on new experiences. Scripts are highly relevant to how we conduct ourselves in relationships. For example, one client, Ray, was convinced that every woman he dated would try to control his life and destroy his spontaneity. His script went something like this:

> *I show a woman I like her. She likes me in return and starts*
> *to talk about commitment. I get anxious. She pushes harder*
> *and starts to demand things from me. Now I really get*
> *anxious and start to disappear. Things go downhill from there.*

Without intending to play out this scenario each time, Ray would find himself under its sway and end up feeling like he had repeated the same mistakes once again. Our work in therapy was to identify this script, but also to connect it to specific memories in his life. The more he could see the script in concrete and emotional terms, the more motivated Ray was to say, "Not again; I have to do something to change this."

As mentioned in earlier chapters, I could help Ray to engage in role-playing and imagining alternate endings in order to break his script's cycle. However, now let us look at how Ray might bring his particular memories and the story he constructs from them to a new relationship.

Imagine that Ray meets Tina and they begin to date. What relationship memories and scripts might Tina have? Tina is someone who has been burned more than once by unreliable and less-than-honest men. Her own script unfolds in the following way:

> *I let the guy know that I have been hurt before and hope he*
> *is different. He assures me he will always be honest and treats*
> *me like a princess. I let my guard down and believe that I*
> *have finally found a true "good guy." I start to do everything*
> *I can to please him. He starts to act bored with me and*
> *indifferent. He ends up cheating on me or breaking it off.*
> *I feel like a fool again.*

Bringing this script to her emerging relationship with Ray, she is likely to be very cautious at first and hold back from commitments and expectations. Ironically, this early behavior is going to pull Ray in and lead him to think that he has found the independent, non-commitment-oriented person that he imagines he wants. Her holding back lures Ray in and causes him to express more and more interest in Tina. As the relationship proceeds in this seemingly positive fashion, both Ray and Tina may not be aware that they have already triggered each other's scripted sequence. Ray's enthusiasm for the relationship eventually weakens Tina's reserve, and she begins to allow her strong need to commit to a "good guy" emerge. Just as she opens her heart in this way and seeks to deepen the relationship, Ray's alarm bell about control and loss of independence will go off. As he pulls back, she will move forward, and the full-fledged sequence of both scripts will take over.

So how indeed might individuals blend these potentially destructive scripts in more positive ways? The next exercise provides suggestions for how couples at the start of their relationships can let each other know their important memories and stories in order to avoid repeating the same old mistakes.

EXERCISE 16: HELPING COUPLES BLEND THEIR STORIES IN POSITIVE WAYS

1. This exercise can be done by you on your own or you might decide to recruit a couples therapist to help facilitate your discussions and keep them moving in a positive and constructive direction. Whatever you decide, the key first step in this exercise is that both members must commit to honest and open sharing of their memories with each other.

2. Next, each member of the couple should take time alone to sit down and write a few specific memories that reflect your greatest disappointments and frustrations in previous relationships.

3. Before sharing the memories with each other, you should also write down your most powerful hopes or desires for the current relationship. In other words, you should list what you want for this relationship that would make it better than any previous relationship you have had.

4. Next, each of you should try to write down what you see as the "typical script" (similar to what I have described above) that plays out in your relationships.

5. Working with a couples therapist or on your own, you must now take time to share each others' memories, goals, and scripts. Make sure that you understand them by asking questions of your partner about their thoughts and feelings with regard to each memory, goal, and script. When they give you answers, make sure to restate their replies and confirm that you heard correctly what they have said to you.

6. With all this information shared (and it may take more than one conversation), you both can decide what steps you might take together to preempt your scripts kicking in and to maximize your chances for achieving the relationship goals that you set for yourselves.

Knowing patterns and articulating your fears cannot guarantee that you will suddenly remove these dangers from your relationship, but it is an honest and constructive step in the right direction. Your partner and you will need to employ patience and communication at every step, but knowing that each of you brings a flawed story in need of repair may invoke the necessary compassion and understanding that will allow a healthier and more satisfying mutual story to emerge.

MIDDLE ADULTHOOD: GENERATIVITY AND GIVING YOUR STORY TO OTHERS

Erikson saw middle adulthood as the period when individuals contemplate the contribution that they are making to the society that they share with others. Erikson called this concern with contribution "generativity" and saw the opposing force as "stagnation" or the sense that one has lived only for immediate needs without any higher purpose or future outcome. As Jonathan Kotre (1984) described in his moving book on generativity, individuals' contributions can come in the form of raising offspring; artistic, intellectual, or civic contributions; or tangible physical products (crafts and handiwork).

Dan McAdams and Ed de St. Aubin (1992) see the generative period of people's lives as the coming together of the two previous life stages—the quest for an independent and unique identity (begun in adolescence) and the search for connection and communion with others (a primary challenge of young adulthood). When we are generative, we simultaneously leave our particular stamp on the world and we make a contribution that connects to others. For example, even raising children, which seems like a purely communal activity, is also an opportunity to carry forward our own values, attitudes, and, in most cases, genetic material.

In considering the connection of generativity to your life story, you can consider the fundamental question of how your own memories can contribute to your offspring (if you are a parent) as well as to the larger society. When we read about the stories of heroic individuals surviving accidents or illnesses, or when we watch film and television stars in roles that depict wrenching adventures or melodramas, it may be a bit daunting to imagine that our own story can be of importance to others. Yet our memories indeed contain lessons and messages that can be highly instructive and useful to others (see chapter 3), not just ourselves. The following exercise helps you to explore ways in which you can put your story to work in the service of your family, friends, and larger community.

EXERCISE 17: GIVING YOUR STORY AWAY

1. In my research on individuals' personal growth, we have studied memories of moments that may be described as rising to the occasion. At such moments, you have faced a challenge or adversity and summoned inner resources to overcome the obstacle and arrive at a better place. Examples of rising-to-the-occasion memories include learning how to live on your own in a foreign country, being given a new set of duties on a job and mastering them quickly, suffering a physical injury or illness and not allowing it to set you back, among many others.

    Using your memory journal, try to write down a few of these rising-to-the-occasion moments from your life. When you see a family member or friend discouraged by a setback and difficult challenge, you might try to console them by providing the example of your own rising-to-the-occasion moment. However, be careful not to do so in a way that promotes a too-positive picture of yourself. Your goal is not to emphasize your accomplishment, but rather to help the other person gain hope and confidence in their abilities to surmount the challenge.

2. A second way of giving your story away is sharing memories with your children of their early lives. We have already discussed in this chapter the great benefits of sharing birth stories with your offspring. Just as importantly, your willingness to talk about other memories from their lives models for children the sequencing of events, details, and emotional responses that characterize a rich and evocative memory. It helps them to reconstruct their own memories and elaborate on them in the healthy ways we discussed earlier.

3. In addition to hearing memories about their own lives, younger children have an almost insatiable curiosity about their parents' lives as children and teenagers. Long car rides are perfect opportunities to share humorous and lesson-teaching memories from your life with your children. These shared recollections are powerful models for them about how you have struggled with the same insecurities, troublesome teachers, and playground bullying that they too have faced or will face in their life.

4. Outside your family, there are increasing outlets for you to share stories of struggle and/or triumph in your life. With the immense growth in self-help and support groups for virtually any kind of physical or psychological difficulty, there are numerous opportunities to exchange stories with others who have undergone similar challenges or crises in their lives. As discussed in earlier chapters, the work of James Pennebaker (1995) has powerfully demonstrated the positive physical and psychological health effects of disclosing difficult and painful memories. In addition to groups that you attend in person, many of my clients and associates have found comfort and helpful information by exchanging personal stories in chat rooms and discussion boards that focus on a particular physical or psychological concern in their life.

Some people find that if they survived an unusual crisis or addressed a life-threatening illness in a successful and enriching manner, then the opportunity to speak to others in a public forum is both salutary for them and generative for others. For example, a friend of mine, Paul, who had weighed well over 250 pounds but was under 5 foot 6 inches tall, underwent gastric bypass surgery and now weighs 145. He has recently put together a PowerPoint presentation to tell the story of the changes he has experienced, both physically and psychologically. He speaks at local schools and community organizations, not for money but to educate people about the surgery and also about societal attitudes regarding obesity and diet. In his talk he relies heavily on personal memories about his life before surgery and then also shares anecdotes about how people responded to his dramatic change in appearance.

In middle adulthood, we have lived out individual stories that express our own unique life paths. However, our daily lives are subject to the powerful influences of family and culture that channel our lives into grooves that have much in common with many others of similar age and background. The memories that we can contribute as testimonies of our distinct experiences are also links to similar worlds of suffering, triumph, and insight that belong to our parents, children, friends, and fellow community members. In giving away our memories, we contribute to this deep sense of connection that defines what it means to share a common society or culture.

LATE ADULTHOOD: WHAT USES DO OLDER PEOPLE MAKE OF MEMORY?

One ageist stereotype in our culture is that people in later adulthood (sixty and over) are prone to live in the past, settling into rocking chairs and front porch swings and talking about "days gone by." Aside from the fact that many older people continue to work well into their seventies, careful research has found that there is quite a variation in how much older people actually engage in life review and intensive scrutiny of their past experiences. Wink and Schiff (2002) reported that only 42 percent of a sample of nearly two hundred older individuals followed over several decades tended to conduct more systematic and deliberate reviews of the events of their lives. Interestingly, individuals who experienced more powerful negative events in midlife (untimely deaths of relatives, divorce, job loss, severe illness) were more likely to have applied themselves to a careful scrutiny of the ultimate integrity and meaning of the choices they had made and the life they had lived. In a not unrelated finding, these researchers also found that older adults who did engage in thoughtful review of the past were more likely to show personality characteristics of openness, creativity, personal growth, and an interest in contributing to the welfare of the next generation.

Of the substantial number of participants from Wink and Schiff's study that did not report life review as an important activity, one should not conclude that they did not engage in any memory of the past. Rather, these individuals tended to recall events from the past as a way of reviving pleasant experiences or as part of shared reminiscences with loved ones.

The emerging consensus in the field of narrative gerontology (the study of how older adults make sense of and describe their past experiences) is that there is a great diversity in how older adults make use of their memories. J. D. Webster (1993, 1997) developed, validated, and replicated a Reminiscence Functions Scale (RFS), sampling over one thousand individuals (ages seventeen to ninety-one) and found eight primary uses of reminiscing, present in both younger and older individuals:

1. **Boredom reduction:** recalling memories for amusement and pleasure

2. **Death preparation:** reviewing life events in order to reach closure before death

3. **Identity:** recalling events to define self and build a sense of unity and purpose

4. **Problem solving:** recalling memories as an aid in generating ideas and solutions

5. **Conversation:** recalling memories for conversational exchange and socializing

6. **Intimacy maintenance:** recalling memories to reinforce shared experiences

7. **Bitterness revival:** recalling memories to brood or worry over unresolved issues

8. **Teaching/informing:** recalling memories to serve as instruction to the next generation

Although older people employ all eight of these reminiscence functions, they were found to be more likely than younger people to engage in the use of memories for death preparation and teaching/informing the younger generation. Let us look at each of these two memory uses in the context of older people's lives.

Death Preparation

In considering this use of memory, I do not want to imply in any way that older adults should live at all times as if death is at the doorstep. My parents, both in their eighties, continue their professional careers at a dizzying pace, publishing books and articles, and jetting around the globe to give speeches, attend conferences, and serve as consultants and board directors. At the same time, they are increasingly recognizing that there is a body of unique experiences stored in their memories that will leave this earth when they ultimately reach their lives' end. Older people, even those still caught up in the flurry of active lives, owe it to themselves and the next generations to ensure that these memories will not be lost. This idea of preserving a legacy of memory for future generations is closely tied to the idea of informing and teaching, so I will address it in the next section of this chapter. However, there is a more self-focused concern for life review that all older people might benefit from considering.

Through our determined efforts to take on the next task and to push forward with future plans, we inevitably put aside and leave unfinished (sometimes literally and sometimes psychologically) important issues in our lives; this unfinished business can involve people, work, community, ethical concerns, and spiritual questions. In reviewing our decisions, choices, or responses to major obstacles or challenges across our lives, we indeed can look for ways to come to a place of acceptance, peace, reconciliation, and closure. Rather than allow lingering doubts or haunting regrets to undermine this phase of our lives where pride in accomplishment and contentment should be paramount, it can be extremely helpful to devote some time to recognition of struggles and then to undertake a kind of cleansing of concern and worry. This kind of careful scrutiny and letting go can free older people to relax and live more in the moment in this phase of their lives, unencumbered by the baggage and preoccupations of the past. Here is an exercise for making peace with those lingering memories of struggle.

EXERCISE 18: MAKING PEACE WITH MEMORY AND LETTING GO

1. In order to free yourself to feel a deeper sense of grace and peace at this juncture in your life, try to identify a particular memory that expresses regret or a feeling of having missed the mark.

2. Write out this memory on a separate piece of paper (not in your memory journal). Write out all the details, thoughts, and concerns that might be associated with the memory.

3. Now, and this is critical to the exercise, you must write down on a second piece of paper any or all of the following statements that apply to the memory that you have described:

    a. Under the circumstances, I did the best that I could.

    b. I am only human and am allowed to make mistakes.

    c. I meant well even if the result did not end up as I wished.

    d. This incident does not capture all of whom I am.

    e. I have punished myself enough for what went wrong.

    f. I cannot change the past and therefore must let go.

4. Take both pieces of paper and fold them together so that you can see that both your troubling memory and your statement of reconciliation are entwined. Now place

them in an envelope and seal the envelope. Write on the envelope the words "Letting Go."

5. Take the envelope, a small metal bucket, and a book of matches to a place of particular peace and beauty in your life. It could be an ocean, river, mountain view, or park.

6. Sit quietly and reflect over the memory and the words of release that you have written down. Repeat the words of release several times (for example, "I cannot change the past and therefore must let go"). Finally, light a match and place it to the envelope inside the bucket and let the envelope fully go up in flames. Tell yourself that the smoke rising from the bucket is the memory leaving from your heart and soul to be replaced by a respectful calm and peace.

7. When there is only cool ash left and there is no trace of spark or glowing cinder, scatter the ashes into the air as a final gesture to support the feeling of letting go.

Each year as summer ends and fall is about to begin, the Jewish people celebrate the end of their calendar year and engage in a week of repentance. The particular holiday of repentance is called Yom Kippur and its highlight is the singing of the ancient prayer of Kol Nidre. As the cantor sings the haunting melody of the prayer, the words plead with God to free all members of the congregations from their oaths and vows and to forgive them for all their sins and transgressions. The prayer recognizes that all humans fall short and miss the mark. We do not live up to values of kindness, honesty, and justice that we set for ourselves, nor do we always succeed in rising above our own self-concerns or petty interests. Yet as the mournful prayer repeats three times, we are carried by its waves of reproach and mercy to an understanding of our own humility and shared fate with each and every other human being. We are ultimately washed clean of our failings and begin the new year with fresh hope for acts of goodness and grace.

The act of letting go of these memories as you prepare for a new phase of the life cycle bears much resemblance to the Jewish rituals of atonement. Regardless of what god you petition or ritual you conduct in order to obtain forgiveness, you must also learn how to forgive yourself and let drop any finger pointed at yourself. Whatever had happened before, this day asks how you will live, and the next day asks the same question, and so on, until you have no more days. Try to let the day that you are living now, and the ones that are still to come, give you peace instead of regret, and hope instead of sorrow.

Teaching/Informing

If you have reached the age of sixty or seventy or eighty or more, you have accumulated a vast body of knowledge and experience. You have earned the right to be called "wise" and the younger generations can benefit from your wisdom. What exactly is wisdom? In their book *Ordinary Wisdom: Biographical Aging and the Journey of Life*, W. L. Randall and G. M. Kenyon (2001) describe six dimensions of wisdom that older individuals have culled from their life experiences:

1. **Cognitive:** expertise and knowledge gained through years of problem solving

2. **Practical-experiential:** knowing the steps to take in life that lead toward peace

3. **Interpersonal:** basing life's essence in the web of relationships with others

4. **Ethical-moral:** placing ultimate value on authenticity and compassion in life

5. **Idiosyncratic expression:** respect for the uniqueness and diversity of life

6. **Spiritual:** the ability to find meaning even in the face of suffering and loss

Randall and Kenyon describe the events that led the Buddha on his journey of spiritual awakening. In immediate succession, he encountered an old person, a sick person, a corpse, and a traveling monk. These four signs moved him to see that beneath decline and death there is always a spiritual essence in place, waiting to be uncovered. All stages of life are part of the journey to this place, a journey that is not along a linear path, but is more an unwinding motion, a circular dance that brings us closer each time, as we return to our starting place, to a higher and more refined truth. If we allow our memories to teach us, and offer their lessons to others as well, we are traveling the same path of wisdom that the Buddha set out on nearly three thousand years ago.

We began this chapter describing the ways in which our mothers recounted our arrival in this world—the literal stories of our birth. We then learned how our families and culture teach us to give a story form to the experiences of our young lives—how to organize the narratives of our memories to include elaboration of details and our emotional responses to events. In adolescence we borrow from the plot structures and prominent characters of our particular society to forge our beginning life stories, our own personal epics that place us in the role of hero facing the imposing challenges of work and love. Young adulthood asks us to blend this newly emerging life story with another person's story, and to find a way of weaving a mutual narrative of intimacy and communion. Middle adulthood sees us well immersed in family, work, and community structures and asks what our distinctive and lasting contribution to each of these defining worlds might be. Now, as we ponder older adulthood, we draw on all the wisdom culled from each of these story-making endeavors, from all the memories engendered, to contemplate how to give back the story into which we breathed our life. For at the end of our lives we come to see that it is indeed a borrowed story that belongs to our offspring and their children, to the community we shared, and to the society in which we participated.

When I was a child my favorite book was *My Friend Charlie*, by James Flora (1964). It was about a small boy who had a friend named Charlie who excelled at everything, including being a great friend. In episode after episode the boy detailed the wonderful ways in which his friend Charlie embellished his life, adding imagination, fun, and excitement. At one point, the boy tells Charlie about a dream he had and Charlie says that it sounds like a great dream and perhaps he could borrow it. The boy lends Charlie his dream and Charlie keeps it and dreams it himself for a few days. When he returns the dream, the boy is amazed by how Charlie has enhanced it, giving it new twists and turns and a cast of fantastic characters.

The way that life stories are born from the interaction of culture and the individual is very much like the story of the boy and his best friend, Charlie. As each human being comes into the world, our culture is like the small boy with a dream. Our culture lends its dream with its fundamental plot and characters to each new Charlie. It does so through the stories parents tell and through the world of media, myths, and literature that rapidly fill each waking and dreaming moment. In turn and with increasing momentum, each unique Charlie in this world takes these borrowed supplies—"the stuff that dreams are made of"—and crafts a unique dream—a life of memories—of his own.

Each individual makes a story that no one has ever lived or could have ever known before. Each story builds to climaxes of desire, triumph, disappointment, and redemption in ways that no one could fully predict or anticipate. Ultimately, every Charlie, every well-meaning neighbor's child, who in total make up what we call a community or society, returns this embellished story—this honed collection of memories, polished, shined, made better than before—to the rest of us. As we take back this story of one individual life that spans from birth to death, we see indeed that it has grown, become richer, taken on more intrigue and depth than we had thought possible, gained more humor and irony, taught us about darker corners and layers of weakness, moved at times toward evil, but also invoked compassion. Each life, if we honor it, is a debt repaid, a history book to instruct us, and an ultimate chronicle of what the theologian Paul Tillich called the "courage to be."

As the final exercise of this chapter, I would encourage you to consider how indeed to be the best possible friend with regard to your memories that you can be. How might you return the story of your life—the collection of your memories—to your family and to the larger community? One answer is to consider the different ways that you could leave a permanent legacy of memories for the next generations to have as a record of your life. Here are some possible concrete steps.

EXERCISE 19:
LEAVING A PERMANENT LEGACY OF MEMORY

1. Imagine you are writing a letter to a great-grandchild or great-grandniece or great-grand nephew (not yet born) whom you might never meet. Divide up your life into major chapters (such as childhood, teen years, early adulthood, middle adulthood, later adulthood, the present time) and select key memories that you might want to share about your life. If you do not have the

inclination to write a more extensive memoir, try to select your most powerful self-defining memories from each period. Touch on some of the major areas of life:

a. Relations with parents, siblings, and relatives; friendships

b. School life; sports, arts, and hobbies; first romantic relationships

c. College or early work years

d. Beginnings of committed relationships

e. Progression in work life

f. Role as caregiver for children, relatives, friends, or community members

g. Leisure activities and travel

h. Spiritual life

i. Retirement or experiences with growing older

Do not worry about the literary value or the polish of these written memories. Anything that you set down will be eagerly devoured by all of your family who have an opportunity to read your reminiscences. For some of you, it might be easier to recall these memories into a tape recorder and less overwhelming than the writing process.

2. If you feel that this process of recalling your memories is too daunting to take on alone, you can ask your adult children to videotape or record you while they ask questions and help to prompt memories. You can use the same categories listed above to get you started.

3. If your family members and you would like assistance in pulling together this living history of your life, there are some exciting new options available through the Internet. A company called Totem Software (www. totem-software.com) will supply you with a software program that connects to a digital video camera and your

computer (in either Mac or PC versions) and guides you through an interview and cataloging process (it provides three hundred possible interview questions to get you started!). It allows you to edit the video on the computer and to assign links and tabs to different segments of the video (for example, you can click on the label "work life" to watch the portion of the interview that covers that topic). The price for the software was $60 at the time of my writing this chapter.

4. If you would like a professional from outside your family to assist you with the collection of your memories and the documentation of your life, I would recommend that you go to the website overseen by the Association on Personal Historians (www.personalhistorians.org). This website lists numerous companies and individuals who specialize in collecting personal histories and documenting them on audiotape, video, and CD-ROMs. For example, the Memory Bank (www.thememorybank.us) will assist you in producing an edited audio- or videotape. Another organization, Modern Memoirs, has a good track record of producing beautifully edited and bound private memoir books, as well as tribute books for lost loved ones.

Finally, if you have lost a loved one and would like to preserve memories and images of them, you could enlist the help of electronic memorial sites (for example, www.virtual-memorials.com or www. memorialsonline.com).

5. These sites will help you to create a lasting memorial that integrates text, photographs, drawings, and other memorabilia into a tasteful and meaningful tribute to a relative, friend, or coworker.

CONCLUDING THOUGHTS

This chapter has taken us on a journey from the startled cries of a newborn all the way to the quiet reflections of an elder contemplating decades of memories across the intervening years. Finally, I would like to share a more personal story to highlight a critical theme of this travel across the life span of memory.

When I was about twelve years old, I stood in front of my mirror in my bedroom. Perhaps I was aware of the rapid changes that adolescence was bringing on and the greater changes that were to come. Perhaps I had just had a frustrating conversation with my parents about some topic that they simply didn't understand (there were many in those years). I remember looking in the mirror and saying distinctly to myself, "You are a kid now, but you won't always be one. Promise that you will remember what it feels like to be one." What I recall wanting at that instant was to feel that I would always know who I was, that I would always be the same person, even when I changed in physical size or became worried about the kinds of things that my parents endlessly discussed (work and chores and finances). I wanted to know that the person I was at that moment would not disappear, would not be swallowed up by the inevitable life of responsibility and seriousness ahead.

It is nearly thirty-five years since that day in front of the mirror. I am more like my parents than I could ever imagine. I hear myself saying phrases to my daughters that my parents said to me in the same tone and with the same exasperation. Sometimes I hear my voice and actually think it is my father's voice. But despite all this change, despite all the ways in which I wear the mantle of adulthood and let it weigh upon my shoulders, I can remember that moment in front of that mirror and am still trying to keep my promise.

Memory is the one strong chain across all the passing days. It is a chain that anchors your sense of self—who you were, who you are, and who you will be. At the same time, it links you to others through shared reminiscence and storytelling. It links you further to your community and culture through common characters, themes, and plots. It holds within it this consistent promise of connection by serving as an ever-vigilant witness to the lives we mutually share. In return for this promise, we must honor memory by preserving it—writing, taping, filming, digitizing—in whatever media available, so that its legacy will indeed live on and its purpose be fulfilled.

There have been many recent films that have made memory, and particularly the problems of memory, a prominent feature. *Memento*, *Fifty First Dates*, *The Eternal Sunshine of the Spotless Mind*, and even the animated feature *Finding Nemo* all feature characters who have had disruptions to their ability to remember. In some cases, the loss of memory is treated for comic effect (*Fifty First Dates* and *Finding Nemo*) and in others with haunting and tragic effects (*Memento* and *Eternal Sunshine*). However, all of these films' focus on memory reflects for me an underlying message—as a society we are increasingly aware of the fragility of memory. In this world of forty-eight-hour news cycles and unceasing televised and computerized images, our ability to retain information and to sort through what information we should consider important (the essence of healthy memory) is increasingly under threat.

In my twenty years of teaching I have noticed that students show less and less concern with the history of the topics that I teach. In my scholarly research I find fewer and fewer authors cite work if it is older than five to ten years since publication. The dizzying pace of our information age asks us to live more and more in the present. Yet this book has sought to demonstrate the limitless value of reaching back to the past, even as we continue to strain forward toward the future.

In memory we can find insight into our goals and their attainment. We can find life lessons and draw wisdom from our experiences. We can use memories to sustain our spirit and counteract our darkest moods. Following in the footsteps of authors and artists, we can tap our memory as a perpetual source of creativity and amusement. Memory can be an aphrodisiac more powerful than any of the much-publicized pills. And finally, it is our familial and communal glue, holding us together through shared experiences and concerns. It has sustained us through the rise and fall of cultures, through wars and holocausts.

In the spirit of this book, it is my most fervent hope for you, and for all of us, that we shall always remember to remember. It is something that is worth promising to each other.

References

Blagov, P. S., and J. A. Singer. 2004. Four dimensions of self-defining memories (content, specificity, meaning, and affect) and their relationship to self-restraint, distress, and repressive defensiveness. *Journal of Personality* 72:481–511.

Borges, J. L. 1999. Funes, his memory. In *Collected fictions*, translated by A. Hurley. London: Penguin. [Original work published 1998.]

Bower, G. H. 1981. Mood and memory. *American Psychologist* 36:129–148.

Conway, M. A., C. W. Pleydell-Pearce, and S. E. Whitecross. 2001. The neuroanatomy of autobiographical memory: A slow cortical potential study of autobiographical memory retrieval. *Journal of Memory and Language* 45:493–524.

Conway, M. J., J. A. Singer, and A. Tagini. 2004. The self and autobiographical memory: Correspondence and coherence. *Social Cognition* 22:495–537.

Demorest, A. P., and I. E. Alexander. 1992. The personal script as a unit of analysis for the study of personality. *Journal of Personality* 60:645–663.

Elkind, D. 1981. *Children and adolescents* (3rd ed.). New York: Oxford University Press.

Emmons, R. A. 1999. *The psychology of ultimate concerns: Motivation and spirituality in personality*. New York: The Guilford Press.

Erikson, E. H. 1959. *Identity and the life cycle: Selected papers.* Oxford, UK: International Universities Press.

———. 1963. *Childhood and society.* 2nd ed. New York: W. W. Norton.

Fivush, R., and E. Reese. 2002. Reminiscing and relating: The development of parent-child talk about the past. In *Critical advances in reminiscence work: From theory to applications,* edited by J. D. Webster and B. K. Haight. New York: Springer.

Flora, J. 1964. *My friend Charlie.* New York: Harcourt, Brace & World, Inc.

Glasser, W. 2000. *Reality therapy in action.* New York: HarperCollins.

Habermas, T., and S. Bluck. 2000. Getting a life: The emergence of the life story in adolescence. *Psychological Bulletin* 126:748–769.

Hayden, J., J. A. Singer, and J. Chrisler. October 2, 2004. The transmission of birth stories from mother to daughter: Mother-daughter attachment, self-esteem, and attitudes toward childbirth. Presented at the annual meeting of the New England Psychological Association, Providence, Rhode Island.

Haley, W. E., D. G. Larson, J. Kasl-Godley, and R. A. Neimeyer. 2003. Roles for psychologists in end-of-life care: Emerging models of practice. *Professional Psychology: Research and Practice* 34:626–633.

Harvey, J. 2002. *Perspectives on loss and trauma.* Thousand Oaks, Calif.: Sage Publications.

Isen, A. M. 1985. The asymmetry of happiness and sadness in effects on memory in normal college students. *Journal of Experimental Psychology: General* 114:388–391.

Joormann, J., and M. Siemer. 2004. Memory accessibility, mood regulation, and dysphoria: Difficulties in repairing sad mood with happy memories? *Journal of Abnormal Psychology* 113:179–188.

Josephson, B., J. A. Singer, and P. Salovey. 1996. Mood regulation and memory: Repairing sad moods with happy memories. *Cognition and Emotion* 10:437–444.

Klinger, E. 1999. Thought flow: Properties and mechanisms underlying shifts in content. In *At play in the field of consciousness: Essays in honor of Jerome L. Singer,* edited by J. A. Singer and P. Salovey. Mahwah, NJ: Erlbaum.

Kotre, J. 1984. *Outliving the self: Generativity and the interpretation of lives.* Baltimore, MD: Johns Hopkins University Press.

Linville, P. 1985. Self-complexity and affective extremity: Don't put all your eggs in one cognitive basket. *Social Cognition* 3:94–120.

Luria, A. R. 1982. The mind of a mnemonist. In *Memory observed: Remembering in natural contexts,* edited by U. Neisser. San Francisco, Calif.: W. H. Freeman.

Lyubomirsky, S., N. D. Caldwell, and S. Nolen-Hoeksema. 1998. Effects of ruminative and distracting responses to depressed mood on retrieval of autobiographical memories. *Journal of Personality and Social Psychology* 75:166–177.

McAdams, D. P. 1988. *Power, intimacy, and the life story: Personological inquiries into identity.* New York: Guilford Press.

———. 1990. Unity and purpose in human lives: The emergence of identity as a life story. In *Studying persons and lives,* edited by A. I. Rabin, R. A. Zucker, R. A. Emmons, and S. Frank. New York: Springer.

———. 1993. *The stories we live by: Personal myths and the making of the self.* New York: William Morrow.

———. 2001. The psychology of life stories. *Review of General Psychology* 5:100–122.

———, and E. de St. Aubin. 1992. A theory of generativity and its assessment through self-report, behavioral acts, and narrative themes in autobiography. *Journal of Personality and Social Psychology* 62: 1003–1015.

Meichenbaum, D. 1994. *A clinical handbook/practical therapist manual for assessing and treating adults with post-traumatic stress disorder (PTSD).* Waterloo, ON: Institute Press.

Moffitt, K. H., J. A. Singer, D. W. Nelligan, M. A. Carlson, and S. A. Uyse. 1994. Depression and memory narrative type. *Journal of Abnormal Psychology* 103:581-583.

Moffitt, K. H., and J. A. Singer. 1994. Continuity in the life story: Self-defining memories, affect, and approach/avoidance personal strivings. *Journal of Personality* 62:21–43.

Nabokov, V. 1966. *Speak Memory.* New York: G. P. Putnam's Sons.

Neisser, U. 1982. Memory: What are the important questions? In *Memory observed: Remembering in natural contexts,* edited by U. Neisser. San Francisco, Calif.: W. H. Freeman.

Nolen-Hoeksema, S. 2000. The role of rumination in depressive disorders and mixed anxiety/depressive symptoms. *Journal of Abnormal Psychology* 109:504–511.

Pennebaker, J. W., ed. 1995. *Emotion, disclosure, and health.* Washington, DC: American Psychological Association.

Pillemer, D. 1998. *Momentous events, vivid memories.* Cambridge, MA: Harvard University.

Proust, M. 1932. *The past recaptured, vol. 7 of 'Remembrance of things past.'* Trans. F. A. Blossom. New York: Albert and Charles Boni.

Randall, W. L., and G. M. Kenyon. 2001. *Ordinary wisdom: Biographical aging and the journey of life.* Westport, CT: Praeger.

Roseman, I. J., and C. A. Smith. 2001. Appraisal theory: Overview, assumptions, varieties, controversies. In *Appraisal processes in emotion: Theory, methods, research,* edited by K. R. Scherer, A. Schorr, and T. Johnstone. Oxford, UK: Oxford University Press.

Roseman, I. J., M. S. Spindel, and P. E. Jose. 1990. Appraisals of emotion-eliciting events: Testing a theory of discrete emotions. *Journal of Personality and Social Psychology* 59:899–915.

Rubin, D. C., T. A. Rahhal, and L. W. Poon. 1998.Things learned in early adulthood are remembered best. *Memory and Cognition* 26:3–19.

Schultz, W. T. 2002. The prototypical scene: A method for generating psychobiographical hypotheses. In *Up close and personal: Teaching and learning narrative methods,* edited by D. P. McAdams, R. Josselson, and A. Lieblich. Washington, DC: APA Press.

Schwartz, D. 1978. *In dreams begin responsibilities and other stories.* New York: New Directions.

Shenk, D. 2003. *The forgetting: Alzheimer's: Portrait of an epidemic.* New York: Anchor.

Singer, J. A. 1990. Affective responses to autobiographical memory and their relationship to long-term goals. *Journal of Personality* 58: 535–563.

———. 1997. *Message in a bottle: Stories of men and addiction.* New York: The Free Press.

Singer, J. A. ed. 2004. Narrative identity and meaning making across the adult lifespan. *Journal of Personality* 74:437-657.

————. 2005. *Personality and psychotherapy: Treating the whole person.* New York: The Guilford Press.

————, L. A. King, M. C. Green, and S. C. Barr. 2002. Personal identity and civic responsibility: "Rising to the occasion" narratives and generativity in community action interns. *Journal of Social Issues* 58: 535–556.

Singer, J. A., and P. Salovey. 1993. *The Remembered Self: Emotion and Memory in Personality.* New York: The Free Press.

Snellings, L. 1995. *Olympic dreams.* Minneapolis, MN: Bethany House Publishers.

Thorne, A. 2000. Personal memory telling and personality development. *Personality and Social Psychology Review* 4:45–56.

Tomkins, S. S. 1979. Script theory: Differential magnification of affects. In *Nebraska symposium on motivation 1978*, vol. 26, edited by H. E. Howe and R. A. Dienstieber. Lincoln, NE: University of Nebraska Press.

Webster, J. D. 1993. Construction and validation of the Reminiscence Functions Scale. *Journal of Gerontology: Psychological Sciences* 48: 256–262.

————. 1997. The Reminiscence Functions Scale: A replication. *International Journal of Aging and Human Development* 44:137–148.

Williams, J. M. G. 1996. Depression and the specificity of autobiographical memory. In *Remembering our past: Studies in autobiographical memory*, edited by D. C. Rubin. Cambridge, MA: Cambridge University Press.

Wink, P., and B. Schiff. 2002. To review or not to review? The role of personality and life events in life review and adaptation to older age. In *Critical advances in reminiscence work: From theory to applications*, edited by J. D. Webster and B. K. Haight. New York: Springer.

Jefferson A. Singer. Ph.D., is professor of psychology at Connecticut College in New London, CT. He received his Ph.D. from Yale University. He has spent the past two decades researching emotionally significant memories and their role in personality. He is a recipient of the Fulbright Distinguished Scholar Award, which has funded his research on self-defining memories at Durham University in Durham, England. He has served as associate editor of *Contemporary Psychology* and is past-associate editor of the *Journal of Personality* and is on the editorial board of the *Review of General Psychology*. He is a Fellow of the American Psychological Association and the 2005 recipient of the Theodore R. Sarbin Award for Distinguished Contributions to Narrative Psychology, given by Division Twenty-Four, the Society for Theoretical and Philosophical Psychology, of the American Psychological Association

Foreword writer **Peter Salovey, Ph.D.,** is the Chris Argyris Professor of Psychology at Yale University and dean of Yale College at Yale University in New Haven, CT.

Some Other
New Harbinger Titles

The Cyclothymia Workbook, Item 383X, $18.95

The Matrix Repatterning Program for Pain Relief, Item 3910, $18.95

Transforming Stress, Item 397X, $10.95

Eating Mindfully, Item 3503, $13.95

Living with RSDS, Item 3554 $16.95

The Ten Hidden Barriers to Weight Loss, Item 3244 $11.95

The Sjogren's Syndrome Survival Guide, Item 3562 $15.95

Stop Feeling Tired, Item 3139 $14.95

Responsible Drinking, Item 2949 $18.95

The Mitral Valve Prolapse/Dysautonomia Survival Guide,
Item 3031 $14.95

Stop Worrying Abour Your Health, Item 285X $14.95

The Vulvodynia Survival Guide, Item 2914 $15.95

The Multifidus Back Pain Solution, Item 2787 $12.95

Move Your Body, Tone Your Mood, Item 2752 $17.95

The Chronic Illness Workbook, Item 2647 $16.95

Coping with Crohn's Disease, Item 2655 $15.95

The Woman's Book of Sleep, Item 2493 $14.95

The Trigger Point Therapy Workbook, Item 2507 $19.95

Fibromyalgia and Chronic Myofascial Pain Syndrome, second edition,
Item 2388 $19.95

Kill the Craving, Item 237X $18.95

Rosacea, Item 2248 $13.95

Thinking Pregnant, Item 2302 $13.95